MANAGING LOCAL GOVERNMENT

Cases in Effectiveness

Charldean Newell, Editor

ICMA

Leaders at the Core of Better Communities

ICMA advances professional local government worldwide. Its mission is to create excellence in local governance by developing and advancing professional management of local government. ICMA, the International City/County Management Association, provides member support; publications, data, and information; peer and results-oriented assistance; and training and professional development to more than 9,000 city, town, and county experts and other individuals and organizations throughout the world. The management decisions made by ICMA's members affect 185 million individuals living in thousands of communities, from small villages and towns to large metropolitan areas.

Library of Congress Cataloging-in-Publication Data

Managing local government : cases in effectiveness / Charldean Newell, editor.
p. cm.
ISBN 978-0-87326-179-1
1. Local government--United States--Case studies. I. Newell, Charldean.
JS331.M27 2008
352.14--dc22
2008039684

Printed in the United States of America
2015 2014 2013 2012 2011 2010 2009 2008
5 4 3 2 1

Contents

Foreword

A casebook is an application of theory. In this particular instance, theory is represented by *The Effective Local Government Manager,* 3rd ed. (2004), the flagship publication from ICMA Press on local government management.

Responding to feedback from academics using *ELGM* for classroom teaching and trainers using it for professional development, ICMA Press is pleased to introduce *Managing Local Government: Cases in Effectiveness,* which applies the theories discussed in *ELGM* to the realities of local government. The new casebook can be used with *ELGM* or as an independent text. A separate, free *Supplement to Managing Local Government: Cases in Effectiveness* is available for those who wish to know "the rest of the story," that is, the actual outcomes of the cases.

The cases are approximations of actual events. Names, places, and dates have been changed to avoid identifying real people or organizations, and the authors were at liberty to alter the story lines to fit the parameters of the book. In every case, however, the decision situations are real-life dilemmas that local government managers have experienced. Each one offers both current and nascent managers the opportunity to think through sticky scenarios. Not all the results are positive for the manager or the community—certainly a possibility in real-world administration—but other cases reflect an effective resolution of the problem.

The ICMA staff was pleased that several contributors to previous casebooks responded to the invitation to submit cases for this one. We are equally pleased to welcome a number of newcomers to the ranks of ICMA authors. Biographical information about the authors and the editor is available at the end of the book. Charldean Newell, editor of *ELGM* and regents professor emerita of public administration at the University of North Texas, graciously agreed to edit this casebook and worked tirelessly to ensure that it complements and expands on the themes of the core *ELGM* text.

ICMA is particularly grateful to the individuals—academics and practitioners—who reviewed the submitted case studies, helped us select which to include in this collection, and made valuable suggestions for improving the selected case studies. These reviewers were James M. Banovetz, professor emeritus of public administration at Northern Illinois University; Linda Barton, city manager of Livermore, California; Naomi Caiden, professor of political science at California State University, Los Angeles; Terry Childers, deputy city manager of College Station, Texas; Craig Donovan, director of the MPA Program at Kean University, Union, New Jersey; Sarah E. Hannah, assistant town manager, Palm Beach, Florida; Willow Jacobson, assistant professor of public administration and government, University of North Carolina at Chapel Hill; Joan Pynes, professor of public administration, University of South Florida; Hardin Watkins, town manager, Garner, North Carolina; and Paul Wenbert, PW Consulting Services in Mesa, Arizona, and a former city manager. This book would not have been possible without their conscientious assistance, and we applaud them for their work and their professionalism.

I trust that you, the reader, will enjoy and be invigorated by *Managing Local Government: Cases in Effectiveness*. You will find that it represents a spectrum of situations in which local government managers find themselves and that it is faithful in depicting the complexity and difficulty of the decision environment.

A number of ICMA staff members contributed to the production of this book: Christine Ulrich, editorial director; Nedra James, publications assistant; Jessica Kemp, production editor; and Will Kemp, designer. Katherine L. George was the freelance copy editor.

Robert J. O'Neill Jr.
Executive Director, ICMA

Preface

Managing Local Government: Cases in Effectiveness is a complementary publication to *The Effective Local Government Manager*. It evolved from earlier ICMA casebooks such as *Managing Local Government: Cases in Decision Making* and topic-specific casebooks on human resources, financial management, and economic development. Indeed, three cases published in earlier decision-making casebooks are included in the present volume because of their continued relevance.

At one point in the history of public administration education, cases were used extensively as a teaching tool. Today, cases continue to be used as a way of linking theory and practice, and they are particularly useful in helping students at all levels develop reasoning skills and judgment that will lead to an effective course of action.

ICMA has developed a set of eighteen practices that are fundamental to effective local government management (see www.icma.org, then Membership support/ Professional development/Management practices). Each case study in this book highlights one or more management practices, so that the student has a device for discussing all sides of an issue and reaching a well-reasoned plan of action to address a particular problem. Thus, for example, a case might call on the reader to find a way to bridge gaps between staff and elected officials or between two groups of citizens.

Case studies are part fact and part fiction. Our authors constructed them for educational purposes and based them on real events, but the cases have been modified both to assure confidentiality and to organize the "facts" in such a way that a spirited class discussion can ensue. Each case provides background material, states the case itself, lays out the decision problem facing the manager, and provides questions for discussion. *Cases in Effectiveness: Outcomes,* a free download available online in the ICMA Bookstore, contains an aftermath for each case that explains the outcome of the situation and poses additional questions for discussion.

Although the instructor-trainer will be the primary facilitator of discussion, most cases also suggest roles that participants can play. A role-playing exercise is often a means of ensuring that class members fully understand the range of options and viewpoints, and it can lead to lively, illuminating discussions. Some of the cases provide roles only for the administrator and the staff so that the simulated discussion will be analogous to a staff meeting. Other cases include elected officials, citizens, and even special interests that broaden the simulation to the entire context of the decision situation. The instructor can add to or subtract from the roles to accommodate the number of class "actors."

Both discussion leaders and participants are urged to visit the ICMA Bookstore online for the free resource "Using Simulations and Case Studies in Class," which was the introductory material to the *Supplement to Managing Local Government: Cases in Decision Making.* The two commentaries, by James M. Banovetz and John J. Gargan, included in this resource remain vital and valid tools for making the best possible use of case studies.

In advance of the class session, class participants should read the case study and give thoughtful consideration to the questions posed in the case. Those questions elaborate the central dilemma(s) of the situation. In organizing a class or workshop, the instructor-leader can consult the two matrices at the beginning of the book. One indicates which cases address particular topics prominent in *The Effective Local Government Manager.* The other addresses the practice areas that are fundamental to the professional development activities of ICMA and to the Applied Knowledge Assessment used by the more than one thousand managers who participate in the Credentialed Manager Program. Not all the topics or practices are covered by the nineteen cases, but most are.

Managing Local Government: Cases in Effectiveness will meet the needs of both practicing managers engaged in professional development and graduate students who aspire to local government careers. Its context is a practical elaboration of *The Effective Local Government Manager.* Thus, the sections of this book parallel those of the basic management book. Having student-participants read the ICMA Code of Ethics with Guidelines, which appears at the end of the book, is a good starting place. The Code is important not only as a guide to managerial behavior and a focus for managerial actions described in the cases but also as an integral part of continuous professional development of ICMA members.

Part I emphasizes the profession of local government managers, including leadership style as well as the realities of leading a manager's life. These topics are found in Chapters 1 and 8 of *The Effective Local Government Manager*. The case studies demonstrate that professional growth and development are an important part of the overall profession of local government. Although ethical dilemmas are posed throughout the book, Part I especially emphasizes the primacy of ethics as the cornerstone of the local government management profession. This section also shows that career progression is sometimes rocky, especially if the wrong decision is made at a critical time.

Part II includes cases showing how a manager can be an effective community leader. These cases demonstrate the importance of understanding the nature of the community and the key players and of adopting a leadership style that fits the jurisdiction. The cases show that many special interests constitute a city or county: the manager must be able to understand and deal with all of them.

Part III explores how a manager can help his or her community governing body become more effective. Amateurism has long been a proudly held feature of council-manager government; that is, the basic theory of the form of government posits that the mayor and council will be part time, leaving the day-to-day operations to the professional manager. However, there is a price to pay for amateurism, including a governing body's easy descent into raw politics. Part III also illustrates the fact that change, even for the most rational of reasons, does not always come easily to a governing body.

Promoting the community's future is the theme of Part IV. Historically, planning for the future was limited to land-use planning, which is still of great importance in local jurisdictions. However, promoting a desirable future involves larger considerations such as citizen participation, strategic planning, managing growth while preserving tradition, and strategies for economic development. Dealing with competing interests is a key part of promoting the community's future.

Part V deals with the nitty-gritty issues of human resource and financial management. No organization succeeds without effective workers and adequate funding, and a manager must tend to the development of both. Often, the manager must juggle considerations of who benefits from a given policy or practice.

Policy implementation, productivity, and program evaluation are highlighted in Part VI. Managers must understand how issues reach the governing body's agenda.

They then must take responsibility for effective implementation of a resulting policy even if they do not fully agree with the policy. Elected officials, increasingly interested in accountability, are tasking managers with developing appropriate measures of organizational effectiveness.

Part VII, the last section, reflects on the complexities that occur when two or more organizations, both governmental and nongovernmental, must address the same problem. For many years, the thinking was in terms of horizontal (local-to-local) and vertical (federal-state-local) relationships, but interorganizational relations is an expanding concept. In today's local decision environment, public entities often deal with private organizations, either nonprofit or for-profit, as well as with other governments.

The editor would like to thank Robert L. Bland, chair of the Department of Public Administration at the University of North Texas, for assistance in preparing Case 16. She thanks Christine Ulrich, editorial director of ICMA, not only for her expertise but also for her ability to induce calm when progress seemed to be inordinately slow. She also thanks the many managers to whom she has posed specific questions in an effort to gain better understanding of various issues as well as Michael St. Pierre, a public administration doctoral student at the University of North Texas, for organizational assistance early on.

—Charldean Newell
Regents Professor Emerita of Public Administration
University of North Texas

Matrix of cases and topics

Subject	Case Number																		
1. Profession of Local Government Management																			
Professionalism	1	2	3						9							16			
Leadership	1	2	3																
Ethical behavior	1	2	3			6		8				12	13					18	19
Career progression	1	2	3		5														
2. Achieving Effective Community Leadership																			
Community characteristics				4	5		7	8			11								
Adapting to community				4	5	6					11								
Community dynamics	1			4	5						11								
Multiple actors				4	5	6				10									
Media relations		2		4		6	7				11				15		17		19
3. Enhancing the Governing Body's Effectiveness																			
Role conflicts	1						7	8	9					14					
Strengthening policy-making capabilities							7	8	9							16			
Work environment						6			9										
Conflict resolution							7	8	9										
4. Promoting the Community's Future																			
Leading planning efforts					5		7	8		10	11							18	19
Economic development										10	11								
Growth versus tradition							7			10	11								
Citizen involvement							7			10	11								
5. Essential Management Practices																			
Human resource management						6						12	13	14		16			
Budgeting and financial management		2						8		10				14		16	17		
6. Policy Implementation, Productivity, and Program Evaluation																			
Agenda setting				4					9					14					
Implementation issues	1											12		14	15				
Monitoring and evaluation														14	15	16			
7. Relating to Other Organizations																			
Horizontal relations					5					10							17	18	19
Vertical relations					5					10								18	
Public-private relations					5											16	17		

Matrix of cases and ICMA Management Practices

Practice	Case Number																		
1. Staff Effectiveness	1	2	3	4	5	6			9			12							
2. Policy Facilitation	1					6	7	8		10	11			14	15	16	17	18	19
3. Functional and Operational Expertise and Planning	1			4					9										19
4. Citizen Service					5		7		9	10	11						17		
5. Performance Measurement/Management and Quality Assurance										10				14	15	16			
6. Initiative, Risk Taking, Vision, Creativity, and Innovation																			
7. Technological Literacy																			
8. Democratic Advocacy and Citizen Participation					5		7		9	10	11							18	
9. Diversity	1							8			11		13						
10. Budgeting														14		16	17		
11. Financial Analysis				4		6		8						14		15			
12. Human Resource Management		2	3	4	5	6			9			12	13	14		16			
13. Strategic Planning										10			13			16		18	
14. Advocacy and Interpersonal Communication			3								11								
15. Presentation Skills																			
16. Media Relations		2		4		6	7				11						17		19
17. Integrity	1	2			5	6	7	8				12						18	
18. Personal Development																			

Part I

The Professional Local Government Manager: Leadership Style

Introduction to Part I

The Professional Local Government Manager: Leadership Style

Classic council-manager government has the following characteristics: a small governing board, elected at large on a nonpartisan basis with a mayor selected by the governing board. The mayor in turn hires a professional manager to run the daily operations of the city or county. Over time, jurisdictions have tinkered with that model to make it fit their individual circumstances. District elections, larger councils in larger jurisdictions, direct election of the mayor, even mayor-manager government have been some of the modifications to the basic form.

Regardless of changes in the form, the most distinguishing characteristic that sets local government management apart from other professions is the primacy of ethical behavior. A chief operating officer of a city or county must gain and hold the public trust. An important component of ethical behavior as defined by the ICMA Code of Ethics (see page 175) is continuous professional development—or the expectation that the manager will keep current in management methods, will be vigilant in subordinating his or her own political views, and will follow policy laid down by elected officials after the manager gives those officials the best possible analysis of the outcomes of various policy choices. A manager is expected at all times to be an effective leader.

The first group of cases emphasizes leadership, ethical behavior, and learning from experience. The case studies demonstrate that professional growth and development are an important part of the profession of local government. Case 1, "Managing without Fear or Favor," describes the difficulties a new manager experiences as she tries to instill professional practices in a community more accustomed to highly political government. She has the twin task of doing her day-to-day job and trying to help the community understand the tenets of the council-manager form of government. She faces issues ranging from entrenched local "favorites" to favors done for political supporters.

Case 2, "No Easy Road to Recovery," presents the dilemma for an honest manager dealing with a dishonest municipal officer and the results of "shutting the barn door after the horse has escaped." The manager finds herself facing a public scandal in the form of an embezzling chief financial officer and confronts two critical realities: a threat to her own job and the recognition that adequate financial management controls were not in place.

The final case study in the section, Case 3, "Cartgate," portrays a manager with a short tenure in office who must discipline a popular, long-term assistant who had wanted the job of city manager. The community has been plagued by corruption and by some unprofessional practices peculiar to the municipality. The assistant city manager openly defies the manager and uses his local popularity as a shield. The city manager finds himself between the proverbial rock and a hard place in dealing with the assistant. The case illustrates that appropriate action does not always have desirable consequences.

The management practice area that is emphasized in Part I is staff effectiveness (practice 1). This practice encompasses coaching and mentoring, team leadership, empowerment, and delegating. The cases also concern practice 18, integrity, which includes personal, professional, and organizational integrity.

1

Managing without Fear or Favor

Craig M. Wheeland and Larry M. Comunale

Background

The township of Fargo, Pennsylvania, was a growing community of 15,000 people in the suburbs of Philadelphia. State law defined Fargo's government structure as a commission form of government using partisan elections to choose the three supervisors in staggered elections. (Voters chose one supervisor every two years.) With no professional manager in place, each board member was responsible for a municipal department and had broad decision-making authority regarding its operations.

Suburban sprawl had brought development pressures to Fargo, affecting residential land use decisions, town center business development, and municipal services. Affordable housing in neighborhoods near the town center had attracted Hispanics to the community, raising tensions among residents as well as claims from the Hispanic community that it was not getting its fair share of township services. Once a community that rarely experienced a contested election, the township now saw stiff competition for seats on the board of supervisors.

Republicans held all three seats on the board, but Democrats seemed likely to win a seat in the next municipal election. Several civic and business leaders had formed a nonpartisan group, Citizens for Effective Government, which complicated the calculations of the two political parties. Although a small group, CEG members were well-known leaders in the community and had the financial resources to pursue their reform agenda. CEG decried the patronage, favoritism, and occasional incompetence of township officials. As a first step toward reform, CEG members unanimously advocated hiring a consultant to study township government. Some CEG members were on record as favoring the adoption of a commission-manager form of government with a code of ethics in a new home-rule charter.

Robert Wagner, a retired business executive and lifelong Republican, was halfway through his first six-year term on the board. He was a popular leader in the community, having devoted many years to volunteer service before his election to the board. Wagner was the leader of a faction in the Republican Party that believed Fargo needed to improve the management of the township government. Some of Wagner's friends, both Republicans and Democrats, were members of CEG, and he had aligned himself with the CEG agenda. Wagner persuaded fellow board member Janet Smith to support him for board chairman instead of voting again for the longest-serving member of the board, James Connor. Smith had won a second term in the most recent election, but only by about one hundred votes, so she recognized the reform agenda was popular. As board chairman and with Smith's support, Wagner believed he could reform Fargo's government on his terms. Wagner also believed that over time he could persuade Connor to support the CEG agenda.

Connor had suspected that Wagner would seek the chairmanship and thus was not surprised when Wagner called to tell him of the arrangement with Smith. Connor expressed his disappointment but did not oppose Wagner's selection. He promised Wagner that he would keep an open mind about CEG's reform agenda, but he was completing his third term and was determined to seek reelection in the next year.

At the next board meeting, Wagner was elected chairman and Janet Smith became vice chairwoman.

Changing the Form of Government

With Wagner presiding, CEG members now began to speak at board meetings, urging the board to hire a consultant to begin the process to change the government structure and rules of operation. Democratic Party leaders and the recent Democratic candidate for supervisor joined the call for reform, advocating the formation of a home-rule study commission.

Although CEG members vigorously proclaimed their nonpartisanship, Connor, his Republican supporters, and even Wagner were alarmed to hear the Democrats take up the form-of-government issue. Wagner and Smith supported hiring a consultant to study the township government structure and operations, as CEG suggested, but Connor continued to defend the status quo. He encouraged his supporters to defend, during public comment, the existing government structure by saying it produced responsive government. Connor further encouraged his supporters to portray the call for reform as an unfair attack on the competence of all municipal employees. He opposed hiring a consultant, saying a consultant was "a waste of money."

Following a 2-to-1 vote by the board, a consultant was hired. Reformers were delighted with the consultant's subsequent report. The consultant recommended hiring a professional municipal manager either by ordinance or by using the state's home-rule charter process to change the government structure to a commission-manager form. The consultant also suggested that the home-rule option would allow the township greater flexibility in addressing problems. If home rule were not pursued, the consultant suggested using the option under the Second Class Township Code to add two members to the board of supervisors by referendum. A five-member board of supervisors would increase representation of community interests. Last, the consultant recommended that an ethics code be added to the charter.

Connor criticized the call for home rule as a way to raise taxes and make government bigger. Defending the work he and his fellow supervisors did in directing department heads, he argued that elected representatives should not transfer their responsibilities to an appointed official. Connor also suggested that an ethics code would create unnecessary and burdensome regulations for municipal officials and employees. He appealed to the trust Fargo citizens had for each other as neighbors living in a community with small-town values.

Hoping to broker a compromise that would secure the support of all factions and deny the Democrats an election issue, Wagner proposed using the ordinance option to hire a professional manager. With some reluctance, the leaders of Citizens for Effective Government endorsed the compromise. Democrats welcomed the idea of a professional manager but continued to advocate for a home-rule charter with a code of ethics. Connor was not persuaded. Wagner and Smith passed the ordinance to create the position of township manager.

Hiring a Professional Manager

After a national search facilitated by a consultant, the commission voted 2 to 1 to hire Susan Harlow to be Fargo's first professional manager. Harlow was well qualified for the position. She had a master of public administration degree, seven years' experience as an assistant city manager in a suburban municipality about twice the size of Fargo, and the enthusiastic recommendations of several highly regarded managers familiar with her work. Harlow had been an ICMA member since graduate school and had attended several state and national conferences over the past seven years to foster her professional development. However, she did not have a background in managing a community with highly partisan elections, a culture of ethical lapses, and a lack of a tradition of professional management. Harlow started working in mid-January of an election year.

During the job search and interview process, Harlow learned the basics about Fargo's politics, government, and community needs. Although she had not worked in Pennsylvania or in a community with partisan elections, she was confident she could work with community leaders effectively. She was impressed with Supervisor Wagner. The appointed township solicitor, Bill Johnson, had a solid reputation, and Harlow felt confident she could work with him. She thought CEG would be a consistent citizen voice to support her while she introduced management improvements. Harlow was concerned about Supervisor Connor's continued opposition to reform and his vote against hiring her. However, she appreciated his telling her in advance that he thought she was well qualified for the position but would vote against her because he felt that Fargo did not need a professional manager. Harlow hoped that in time her performance would change his mind about the value of professional management.

Starting a New Job

During her first six months on the job, Harlow learned that the culture of the government and community was not going to change simply because the board of supervisors voted to hire her. Over those six months, Harlow encountered situations and general expectations that challenged her professional identity.

In her first week on the job, Robert Wagner, the board chairman, invited Harlow to attend a dinner being held to honor the long-serving chair of the Republican Party in Fargo. The invitations had been sent prior to her employment, and Wagner thought the dinner would be a good place for her to meet individuals active in the community. Harlow thanked Wagner for the invitation but declined, explaining that the partisan character of the event precluded her attending. Wagner said he understood, apologized for putting her in the position of having to decline, and assured her that he fully supported her adhering to the ICMA Code of Ethics because "that is why we hired you."

Harlow spent the first weeks in her new job meeting with staff during the day and attending various Fargo board, commission, and committee meetings in the evening so she could meet all the citizen volunteers. She offered to meet with community groups as part of her effort to get to know them and explain her role as a professional manager. Harlow was pleased with the complimentary profile published in the weekly newspaper that covered Fargo. The editorial appearing in the same issue also was highly positive. At a subsequent board meeting, Connor remarked that the manager was receiving more publicity and credit than the elected officials.

The morning following her first visit with the planning commission, Harlow found a voice-mail message from Donald Evans, the newly appointed chairman of

Fargo's planning commission. He called to have his name added to the "snow list." Harlow did not understand the message and asked her administrative assistant about it. Then she spoke with the public works director about it. She learned that the snow list contains names of the city officials who are entitled to have the township plow their driveways after a major snowstorm.

Harlow knew that plowing private driveways was the kind of favoritism that fueled citizen complaints. She wanted to end the practice but before doing so sought the advice of the city manager for whom she had worked prior to her Fargo job. On his suggestion, she met with Wagner to review the snow-list practice and provided the entire board a memo explaining the rationale for the new policy, which would prohibit the plowing of private driveways by municipal employees during work hours as well as the use of municipal equipment to plow private driveways at any time. She also sent a letter to the officials on the list to inform them about the new policy, thank them for their service, and welcome any questions. Harlow noticed quiet stares at meetings from some of the officials, but no one said anything negative to her about the change.

A few weeks later, Supervisor Wagner called to inquire whether the township had enough salt in the storage shed for the winter. He said he noticed the supply seemed a bit low when he stopped by the public works garage for a bucket of salt for his sidewalk. Harlow was stunned to learn that Wagner was taking salt from the township supply for his personal use, but she said nothing. She told Wagner she would check on the salt supply with public works.

In March, Harlow learned that two employees in the department of parks and recreation were selling tickets to other township employees for a dinner celebrating Supervisor Janet Smith's reelection. Harlow met with the employees to find out why they thought it appropriate to engage in political activity at work. She learned that other employees did the same thing for their candidates and no one thought it a problem. She decided to issue a clear memo announcing zero tolerance for such political work. When she informed the board during a board meeting, Wagner and Smith fully supported her policy. Smith apologized for the overenthusiasm of her supporters. However, she appeared slightly defensive, explaining that the employees were longtime friends and that she never pressured anyone to either sell or buy tickets on her behalf. Connor simply sat silently shaking his head. During the public comment period at the board meeting, several citizens including Democratic leaders complained about the employees' conduct and thanked Harlow for her actions. On the way out the door after the meeting, Connor sarcastically thanked both Harlow and Wagner for handing the Democrats an election issue "on a silver platter."

The Decision Problem

As she began her sixth month on the job, Harlow believed she had the full support of Wagner and Smith. During the public comment period at board meetings, CEG members praised her for initiating the management audit that was nearly completed. She planned to use the management audit as a foundation for establishing professional personnel relations, a citizen-service orientation, and improved information management. Although Supervisor Connor seemed to keep his distance from her, she thought he might recognize the value of her performance.

Thus she was unprepared for the week that began with a meeting Connor had scheduled with her to discuss upcoming agenda items.

The Monday Meeting with Connor

Harlow's worst fears came true. At their meeting, Connor complained about the change in the plowing policy. He said he gave so much time to the community—as do the citizens volunteering to serve on boards, commissions, and committees—that the least the township can do is plow their driveways. He stated that Wagner and Smith were not "pure as the driven snow," as they liked to portray themselves, and he could provide proof of that if Harlow wanted. Connor also thought Harlow went too far in restricting the political activity of employees and that she infringed on their rights as citizens to participate in Fargo politics. He concluded by saying that the management audit was really a way for her to help the Democrats defeat him in the November election. He urged her to go more slowly on her reform agenda.

Harlow listened to Connor patiently. She assured Connor the changes in policy and the management audit would in time produce efficient, effective, and fair government for the citizens of Fargo with or without him. Harlow pointed to the ICMA Code of Ethics hanging on the wall behind her desk to emphasize that she was nonpartisan. As Connor stood to leave, he said he knew Harlow had registered to vote as a nonpartisan, but he also knew that as an undergraduate she had earned academic credit working on a Democratic candidate's campaign. He left the office telling Harlow her position was a waste of taxpayers' money.

The Tuesday Board Meeting

During public comment at the board meeting the next day, several Democrats suggested that, based on the recent conduct of parks and recreation employees and the issue concerning the snow list, hiring a professional manager was not enough. They praised Harlow's work but stressed that more needed to be done to change the culture of favoritism in Fargo. They renewed their call for a home-rule study commission to create a charter with a code of ethics so "good government" would not depend on the efforts of the township manager. As the meeting continued, Connor asked Harlow if she agreed with the Democrats' comments. Harlow was caught off guard by the question. Before she answered, Wagner intervened and suggested the matter would be best discussed at the next meeting, when it could be placed on the agenda after everyone had time to prepare his or her comments.

The Wednesday Meeting with Chief Cleary

On Wednesday, Police Chief Richard Cleary, who was one of Harlow's biggest supporters, asked Harlow to hire his son as a police officer. Recently returned from a tour of duty in Iraq, his son had been promised a position in the police department, just like the public works director's son who was hired a year ago. Asked the name of the person who had promised his son the position, Cleary said all the supervisors had promised the job at his son's emotional going-away party. He added that all the supervisors had helped people get jobs with the township over the years. Harlow scheduled an appointment to meet with Cleary and his son the following week but did not say how she would respond to the request. After Cleary left, Harlow reminded herself of tenet 11 in the ICMA Code of Ethics, regarding handling "all matters of personnel on the basis of merit." If only it were that simple!

The Thursday Interview Request

As if things could not get worse that week, on Thursday, Sally Mansfield, the newspaper reporter covering Fargo, e-mailed Harlow, asking for a convenient time to meet for a lengthy interview. Sally explained she was working on a feature story about political reform in Fargo. She also wanted to clarify rumors that Harlow was helping Democrats. Harlow decided to wait until Friday morning to respond to Sally's e-mail to give herself time to think of the appropriate way to handle the interview.

The Friday Crisis of Confidence

Sitting in her office Friday morning, contemplating the requested interview, Harlow reflected on the admonition she once heard a city manager give at a conference: "You never have more authority than the day you walk into your office." Harlow now understood exactly what he meant. Despite all of her efforts, problems continued to arise, challenging her ability to manage township affairs without fear or favor. Under the stress of the week's events, Harlow found herself considering whether she should resign.

Discussion Questions

1. Did Harlow err in making a unilateral management decision to end the "snow list" based on tenet 1, tenet 3, and tenet 10 of the ICMA Code of Ethics, instead of asking the commissioners to discuss and vote formally on an ordinance establishing a new policy?
2. Should Harlow meet privately with Chairman Wagner to discuss recent events? Did Harlow err in not confronting Wagner about taking salt to use on his sidewalk?
3. Are there citizens or officials in the township whom Harlow should consult? Who else should Harlow consult?
4. Would Harlow violate the ICMA Code of Ethics if she endorsed the creation of a home-rule study commission?
5. What consequences might arise if Harlow agrees to hire Chief Cleary's son? How could the management audit provide a way for Harlow to manage that request?
6. The commissioners apparently promised to hire Cleary's son before they decided to pass an ordinance to hire a professional manager. Is it ethical to renege on that promise?
7. Should Harlow mention Cleary's request during the interview with Sally Mansfield? What should Harlow say during the interview about rumors and reform in Fargo?
8. Does Harlow need a home-rule charter with a code of ethics to transform the expectations and practices in Fargo government?
9. Under the circumstances, would Harlow violate tenet 4 of the ICMA Code of Ethics if she resigns?

Suggested Simulation Roles

Susan Harlow, township manager
Robert Wagner, supervisor and chairman
Janet Smith, supervisor and vice chairman
James Connor, supervisor
Richard Cleary, police chief
Sally Mansfield, newspaper reporter

2

No Easy Road to Recovery

Victoria Gordon

Background

On a pleasant Saturday afternoon, John Martin, the chief financial officer of the city of Oakdale, was cleaning out the gutters on his house. He waved at the city police car that drove by his house even though he could not tell which officer was in the car. As he took the wheelbarrow full of leaves and debris to the disposal bin near the curb, he was surprised to see the police car parked at the end of the block and even more surprised to see two unmarked cars parked there too. Before he had time to wonder what was going on, a man in a dark suit approached him and asked if he was John Martin. When he replied in the affirmative, the gentleman identified himself as an FBI field investigator and proceeded to arrest John Martin on federal charges of embezzlement.

Meanwhile, down at Oakdale city hall, City Manager Reva Reed, City Attorney Tad Walsh, and Chief of Police Derek LaBelle were putting the finishing touches on the press release that they would issue momentarily. A short while later the city manager and police chief made official statements on behalf of the city, but they refused to answer any questions posed by a local reporter, Erica Fenmore, beyond the content of their prepared statement. It did not take Fenmore long to start contacting local elected officials by telephone. Despite warnings from the city attorney and the FBI to the mayor and council, speculative statements were made to the media by council members as to whether other employees were involved in wrongdoing. The risk of jeopardizing the case against the CFO was ignored by everyone except the mayor.

On Monday morning, the atmosphere at city hall was dismal. City Manager Reed called a meeting with all employees, but under advice of counsel she could not openly share any meaningful details. She assured them that the city would survive this terrible blow and advised them to go about their normal routines in the professional manner she knew they were capable of demonstrating. Despite the encouraging words of the city manager, the morale of city employees was at an all-time low. Everyone felt hurt and betrayed by the CFO's arrest and thought that citizens would no longer respect or trust city employees. Some could not believe that their good friend John Martin could be guilty of any wrongdoing. Many employees could point to times when John had stepped in to help them with both professional and personal problems. Although not admitting any wrongdoing initially, the accused CFO stated publicly that his actions should not be a reflection on the elected leadership of the city or the city manager. Unfortunately, this did little to help the situation at city hall or the morale of city employees.

In the weeks that followed, intense media scrutiny of Oakdale city hall continued as the case against the CFO unfolded.

The Case

City Manager Reva Reed and Mayor Chandler Dixon had a good working relationship. Reed had held her position with the city of Oakdale for the past ten years. She had also served as city manager in two other midsize cities in the region and had come to this position with a stellar reputation. In total, she had served for more than twenty-five years in local government management positions. Although new to politics, the mayor came from a local family with a long history of public service in the community. The other council members had served longer in their respective positions, and disagreements often ran deep but were seldom acrimonious.

The city manager's relationship with the CFO, John Martin, was no different from her relationships with other department heads. Martin was organized and professional and had good working relationships with his staff members. After many years in the private sector, he had started working for the city about five years before Reed was hired. Until she learned of the suspected embezzlement, Reed had no reason to doubt Martin's professionalism, honesty, ethics, or integrity.

The embezzlement had been brought to light by a new finance department employee who noticed an accounting discrepancy in one of the municipality's special revenue accounts and called the bank to inquire about it. The bank provided a copy of the canceled check to the finance department employee, who quickly noticed a much bigger problem involving the endorsement on the check. The bank, after a few more days of looking into questionable deposit transactions, called City Manager Reed, and she in turn called Police Chief LaBelle. Reed's next call was to Mayor Dixon.

Chief LaBelle almost immediately brought the FBI into the investigation process. However, the city manager and mayor were advised to carry on as usual while the FBI investigated Martin so that the CFO would not be tipped off. Two days before the arrest was made, the full city council was informed of the charges that would be made against the CFO, and they were told by the FBI that it did not appear anyone else was involved. Again, the FBI requested that nothing be done or said to alarm Martin.

However, once the arrest was made, it became apparent there would be no business as usual. The council wanted answers and assurances that nothing similar could occur in the future. Irate citizens monopolized every public meeting, impeding the resolution of even routine agenda items. The mayor and council were bombarded at home with calls from citizens demanding a change in top management.

As the investigation evolved, it was revealed that the CFO had been embezzling from the city for more than twelve years—nearly since the time he was hired—by simply bypassing the accounting system. Even though all city accounting and bank records did not date back that far, the investigators were able to assemble enough information to substantiate the length of time of this abuse. The amount of money that had been embezzled was harder to pinpoint.

Essentially, the CFO used his position to misappropriate payments made to the city: he diverted incoming checks to a special bank account that he had set up under the name of an existing city entity. The account was set up at a bank that was not the main bank for city accounts, although it did handle some of the city's business. The checks were never entered into the city's financial accounting system. Bank statements were sent to the CFO at a post office box under the name of a property controlled by the entity. The diverted checks were for a tax that businesses paid quarterly to the city. The revenue fluctuated from year to year; therefore, no red flags were raised for the city or its auditors when that particular fund showed fluctuating revenues. The CFO diverted checks randomly: some checks were for very small amounts, others for more substantial amounts—again, a pattern that did not raise red flags for the bank. This fact made it difficult to discover how much money had been taken. However, it was soon evident that even a conservative figure topped several million dollars.

In the weeks following the arrest, staff members introduced procedural changes that would prevent mishandling and misappropriation of funds in the future. Council members pledged to work tirelessly to prevent future abuses of the system. There was also a call to rewrite and strengthen the city's code of ethics. Additionally, there was strong criticism of the city manager, Reva Reed, and her lack of knowledge that such problems existed. Although the council initially had not taken a formal position on the public criticism of the city manager, as time went on it became evident that the council was split on whether to ask for her removal. Two members placed an item to discuss this issue on the agenda. Mayor Chandler Dixon was outraged and thought that such an unfounded action would only harm the city's already compromised reputation.

As the next council meeting approached, City Manager Reed found herself facing vocal pressure from the council to resign or retire or to risk being fired. In considering her situation, she also considered the problems the city faced—finding her replacement, replacing the ousted CFO, securing changes to the handling of revenues, and rebuilding employee morale.

The Decision Problem

With the discussion of her leadership on the agenda for the council meeting to be held in two days, the city manager had 48 hours to decide how to proceed. Should she force the council to fire her—or resign? If she gave into the demands of the council to leave, what message would her resignation or "retirement" send to the citizens, to the honest people who worked for the city, to the mayor and council members who supported her, to other cities within the region, and to state officials? Conversely, what message would her dismissal send? If she decided to leave, what should her next step be? Could she leave her job with the assurance that the city employees and the public would be involved in selecting her replacement in a way that would help to restore public confidence and raise the morale of the employees? How could she lead the city, the council, and the citizens through this difficult time if she decided to leave?

As Reed thought through her alternatives, her first instinct was to stay put and force the council to decide whether to fire her. However, she knew that if faced with being forced out, she would much rather resign or retire on her own terms. She then would be able to make some suggestions to the mayor that might ease the transition. For example, she could ask the mayor to name an interim city manager, perhaps by drawing on the expertise of an ICMA Range Rider or suggesting a promotion of someone from within to the position of interim city manager. Additionally, she could suggest the hiring of an outside consulting firm to help with the selection process of a new city manager.

Reed was too wise not to realize that she was replaceable. Her reluctance to leave was grounded partly in the knowledge that this problem had occurred on her watch and partly on her desire not to abandon the city. Whether or not this was a rational assessment of the situation, she felt an overwhelming sense of responsibility to fix the myriad problems that had surfaced as a result of the arrest of the CFO. The clock was ticking. What should she do? What would she do?

Discussion Questions

1. What competing values are in conflict as Reva Reed, the city manager, makes her decision?
2. What should Reed do? What would you do in her situation? Are there alternatives that she is overlooking? What previous actions might she have taken? Would the ICMA Code of Ethics with Guidelines offer any assistance to the city manager as she makes her decision? Is there one correct ethical course of action that presents itself to you, given what you know of the case?
3. Assuming Reed resigns, is her desire for post-resignation control over subsequent events justified? Is there a time when a person in a difficult situation needs to just let go and move on?
4. If we assume City Manager Reed was not legally culpable for the crimes committed by the CFO, does that assumption help you to decide what her course of action should be? Conversely, if we assume that she was legally culpable for not adequately supervising the actions of the CFO, does that change your decision?
5. What were some of the obstacles and opportunities that you identified to solve the decision problem?
6. Would the city's reputation be harmed whether or not Reed left? Would it be hurt less if the city manager resigns or if she is fired? Would you expect the damage to be short term or long term?
7. For a city manager, what are the advantages and disadvantages to resigning, to retiring, and to being fired? What severance provisions might her employment contract include?
8. If Reed had the option to retire—eligibility in terms of years on the job and her age—and her future employment was not of concern, how might that affect her decision?
9. In general, what can we learn from the experiences of those involved in this case?

Suggested Simulation Roles

Reva Reed, city manager
Chandler Dixon, mayor
John Martin, chief financial officer
Derek LaBelle, chief of police
Tad Walsh, city attorney
Erica Fenmore, newspaper reporter

For an expanded role-playing exercise, additional roles could include the local FBI agent, an outraged citizen, a representative of the city's employees, and members of the city council.

3

Cartgate

Susan M. Opp

Background

Lakeview is a medium-sized city in a rapidly growing region in the southeastern United States. The city has a typical council-manager form of government with five council members and a city manager appointed by the council. The council is headed by an elected mayor with strictly ceremonial duties. Lakeview's residents are unusually active in local politics and are frequently active, vocal participants in meetings.

Over the past decade Lakeview has faced high population growth and increased crime. During this same time the city government has been accused of waste, inefficiency, and corruption. Increasingly unhappy with the status quo, citizens turned to their elected officials for some change and accountability in their government. In response, the city council fired the long-standing city manager.

Although the city council laid most of the blame for the corruption and waste on the city manager's office, the deputy city manager did not face the same level of scrutiny as his boss. In fact, Tom Gilchrist was well respected by citizens and regarded as a hardworking, highly skilled administrator. He was personable: most city employees really liked him both as a person and as a boss. He was a lifelong Lakeview resident and had worked his way up from an entry-level public works position to his current post. When the city manager was fired, Gilchrist hoped to be promoted to the now vacant position.

Under state law public positions must be advertised for a period of at least six weeks before being filled. Knowing that this requirement prevented an immediate selection of a new city manager, Gilchrist applied for the position and waited confidently to be selected as the new city manager of Lakeview.

However, as applications came in for the vacant position, council members began to realize that Gilchrist was not the best fit for the position. Although he was experienced, he had little formal education. Furthermore, some council members began to associate him with the old way of doing things under the previous city manager and suspected he would fail to make changes that the citizenry demanded. As a council election loomed in the not-too-distant future, the city council began to view the search for a new city manager as an opportunity to secure its own future in Lakeview.

Introducing the New City Manager

Among many fine applicants, one seemed to be the answer the community was looking for. Grant Albert was a city attorney from a large city in a neighboring state. Albert had served in that position for more than ten years and had won multiple public service awards for his efficiency, effectiveness, and abilities. Prior to becoming a city attorney, Albert served the country in a successful military career and obtained a juris doctorate, a master of law degree, and a master of public administration degree. The city council believed his no-nonsense attitude, experience as an attorney, education, and high recommendations made him just what Lakeview needed to curb the waste, inefficiency, and corruption. Albert was hired as Lakeview's new city manager.

Cleaning Up Lakeview

Grant Albert came to Lakeview with the goal of cleaning up the city's government and saving the taxpayers some money. Albert was able to use his training as an attorney to quickly identify and terminate several longtime city employees who were violating the law and wasting taxpayers' money for personal benefit. His quick action saved the city hundreds of thousands of dollars. Council members were confident they had made the right decision and felt sure of their victory in the upcoming elections. However, Albert's no-nonsense attitude and eye for waste, along with the sweeping changes he made in the various city departments, won him few friends among department heads.

As time passed, Albert continued to run the city in a strict, no-nonsense manner, and no employee was spared his scrutiny. He tolerated no waste and expected employees to perform their duties in a professional and efficient manner. For the most part, Albert was extremely pleased with the city's progress. However, one area began to frustrate Albert: the ability—or in this case, the perceived inability—of the deputy city manager. Although Gilchrist was well liked in the city, Albert thought he was overpaid and underqualified for the second-in-command position. For his part, Gilchrist was obviously angry about being passed over for the city manager position and displayed an unprofessional attitude. Since Grant Albert's arrival, Gilchrist made a point of going home at five o'clock and never working on weekends. Albert questioned his commitment to the city.

The crisis came on the Fourth of July. Every year, Lakeview sponsored a large lakeside fireworks display to celebrate the holiday. In past years both the city manager and the deputy city manager took a paid holiday break. However, in line with his managerial style, Albert decided that both he and his deputy city manager should work the holiday, monitoring the celebrations for code enforcement. It had been an unusually dry year, and the fire danger from unauthorized or improperly detonated fireworks was high. In addition to the efficiency gains from working the holiday, Albert thought that he and Gilchrist could provide a good example of hard work and commitment to the citizens of Lakeview. Besides, the fire and police officers never had the holiday off and neither should the two highest ranking city employees, he believed.

Gilchrist was upset about being forced to work on the holiday. As the father of two children, he thought his time was better spent enjoying the holiday with his family. He challenged the request that he work the holiday and wrote a memo to his boss.

Memorandum

July 1
To: Grant Albert, City Manager
From: Tom Gilchrist, Deputy City Manager
Re: July 4th Holiday

(continued)

I am writing this memo to formally request the 4th of July holiday off from code enforcement duties.

Although I understand the importance of efficiency and hard work, I feel that being requested to work the 4th of July holiday is both unfair and unnecessary. In my fifteen years with the city of Lakeview I have never worked a 4th of July holiday and do not think my presence is needed this year. My two daughters truly enjoy this holiday, and it is a family tradition for us to spend the day at the lake together watching the fireworks.

I respectfully ask that you reconsider the working schedule for the holiday.

Thank you for your time.

Albert responded to the memo with a note of his own.

Memorandum

July 2
To: Tom Gilchrist, Deputy City Manager
From: Grant Albert, City Manager
Re: Memo Dated July 1

I am in receipt of your memorandum dated July 1st re the July 4th holiday. As I stated in our meeting on June 25, it is essential that the City Manager's office demonstrate the hard work and commitment we have to the city of Lakeview. Part of this commitment involves working undesirable dates and times. I do not feel that your request to take July 4th off is appropriate or necessary. You are expected at the lakefront promptly at noon for code enforcement. You will still be paid your holiday pay rate–but are expected to work.

The Fourth of July

The Fourth of July brought more than a million individuals to the lakefront of Lakeview. Grant Albert worked hard to meet, greet, and supervise the various citizens, vendors, and fireworks personnel. Although it was crowded at the lakefront, Albert was surprised not to see Tom Gilchrist all day and asked him about it after the holiday. Gilchrist told his boss that he had in fact worked the entire day at the lake and reported nothing unusual about the day. Not satisfied, Albert asked some of the department heads whether they had seen Gilchrist during the celebrations. Two days later Albert received the following note:

July 8

Dear Grant:

In reference to your inquiry, I wanted to let you know that Tom was working on July 4th. At approximately 12:30 p.m. I received a call from Tom requesting that I meet him at the municipal golf course. At 1:00 p.m. I turned over a city-owned golf cart for Tom to use in his code enforcement duties. The golf cart was returned to our course the following morning by Tom.

Respectfully,
Sandy Moore, Manager of Lakeview Golf Course

Albert had not authorized the use of a city-owned golf cart and wondered why the deputy city manager would need one to carry out his code enforcement duties. The lakefront was too crowded for a golf cart to be of use.

Upon further inquiry Grant Albert discovered evidence that Tom Gilchrist had spent a large part of the day transporting his children, his children's friends, and his spouse from his home to the lakefront in the city-owned golf cart. Additionally, one resident reported seeing Gilchrist's teenage daughter driving the golf cart when Gilchrist was not present. In light of these findings, the city manger promptly suspended Tom Gilchrist with pay, pending further investigation.

The Investigation

Over the next two weeks, City Manager Albert interviewed city department heads, police officers, and citizens concerning the activities of Tom Gilchrist on the Fourth of July. He also solicited a detailed report of activities on the day in question from Gilchrist himself. Gilchrist's account of the day's events was made public.

> On July 4th of this year I, Tom Gilchrist, was requested by the city manager to perform code enforcement duties for the city of Lakeview. I have faithfully worked in this city for over fifteen years and truly love this community and the residents of it. Typically I spend the holiday with my wife and children and was very disappointed that I would be unable to do that this year. I respectfully asked for the day off, but, in keeping with his hard-liner and inflexible attitude, Albert demanded that I work the holiday. Perhaps in a show of poor judgment, I requested a city-owned golf cart from the municipal golf course. I used that golf cart to take my family from our home to the lakefront for the holiday. Our home is only four blocks from the lakefront, and during the drive to and from my home I interacted with community members as Albert requested of me. I can assure you that at no time did I allow anyone else to drive the golf cart. I spent very little time away from the lakefront and did observe activities of the community members during the celebration to ensure that no illegal activities or code violations occurred. I do apologize for my lack of judgment in the use of city property and can assure you and the residents of this community that I will not repeat this mistake.

In addition to compiling witness statements, Albert researched the laws and rules surrounding the misuse of public property. His findings indicated that the deputy city manager violated numerous state laws, local ordinances, and personnel policies. The most egregious violations were the solicitation of gifts (requesting public property under false pretenses), misusing public property by allowing someone else to use the golf cart, lying to the city manager about his actions on the day in question, and failing to perform his assigned duties.

City Politics

Angry at his boss for suspending him, Gilchrist spent much time during the course of the investigation discussing his situation with various friends in the community. Phone calls and more than 200 letters rolled into the city council members' offices—calls and letters supporting Tom Gilchrist and expressing displeasure with the city manager's handling of the Fourth of July incident. Letters also flowed in to the local paper, and citizens began to refer to the incident as Cartgate.

With elections just a few short weeks away, the city council began to get nervous about the public outcry over the deputy city manager's suspension. Lakeview's mayor sent the following letter to the city manager.

> Dear Grant:
>
> It has come to the council's attention that you have suspended your deputy city manager for activities surrounding the 4th of July. It is our position that although Tom Gilchrist's actions that day showed poor judgment, suspension of him is an overreaction and is costing the city important work time. We respectfully ask that you consider lifting his suspension and allow him to return to work. Gilchrist has been a faithful employee of Lakeview for over fifteen years and is an important asset to this community.
>
> Respectfully yours,
> Sharon Collins, Mayor

Investigation Complete

Although Grant Albert was impressed by the public support for Tom Gilchrist, he felt he must not deviate from his standard operating procedure. Albert thought that a city manager has the inherent duty not to be swayed by politics and to act in the best interest of the community. Given Gilchrist's violation of law, ordinance, and personnel policy and his apparent disregard for managerial authority, Albert thought the only suitable penalty was termination of employment: Tom Gilchrist was a liability to the city and to the citizens of Lakeview. His actions could have cost Lakeview thousands of dollars. Two weeks after his suspension, Tom Gilchrist was terminated from his position as deputy city manager. In accordance with standard policy, he was given six weeks to file an appeal with the city's civil service board.

As word of the termination of the deputy city manager spread throughout Lakeview, many citizens and public employees protested the action. Letters poured in to the editor of the local newspaper, to the city council members, and to Grant Albert. City council members grew increasingly worried about their chances of reelection and about Albert's management style.

Appeal to the Civil Service Board

Tom Gilchrist immediately filed an appeal of his termination with the Lakeview civil service board. After several weeks of preparation and document presentation by both sides, the appeal meeting began.

The board heard testimony and reviewed documents for more than a week. In total, 22 hours of testimony were heard and hundreds of pages of documents were reviewed. At the end, the board found in favor of Tom Gilchrist and recommended his reinstatement. As the head of the board stated, "Given Tom's record with the city, the punishment didn't fit the crime, because Tom never denied he used poor judgment." The board further recommended that Tom Gilchrist's personnel record be expunged of all references to Cartgate.

Although the civil service board's decision was in favor of Tom Gilchrist, under Lakeview's city charter, its findings can serve only as an advisory recommendation to the city manager. The city manager ultimately has the power to accept as is, modify, or outright reject the recommendation.

The Decision Problem

Only a few months earlier, Grant Albert was widely viewed as a successful city manager who had succeeded in cutting waste and promoting efficiency in Lakeview. Now he was facing an unhappy city council, citizen outcry, and a civil service board that decided against him. Grant Albert now had to decide how to handle the situation in view of the political and public pressure to reverse a decision he felt strongly was the right one. He feared for his own future, realizing this decision was extremely important to the city and his own career.

Albert spent the next several days thinking about his problem and trying to make the right decision based on the facts and what was best for the community. He identified several options.

1. He could do the politically popular thing: accept the recommendation of the civil service board and reinstate Tom Gilchrist as deputy city manager. Given Gilchrist's dislike of Albert and disregard for his authority, Albert worried about the long-term implications of such a decision. Additionally, he worried that reversing his decision would open the door to future challenges to his judgment.
2. He could stick with his initial decision to terminate Tom Gilchrist, even though he would likely face an extremely unhappy city council and possibly even lose his own job when his contract came up for renewal next year.
3. To attempt a compromise, he could offer Gilchrist his previous position as director of public works. Such a demotion would cut Gilchrist's salary by more than $25,000 and would likely be viewed as an insult. However, the demotion would keep Gilchrist in Lakeview while nevertheless penalizing him and also free Albert to select a better qualified deputy city manager.

Grant Albert's decision will affect Lakeview's future and his own as well.

Discussion Questions

1. One of the perceived benefits of the city manager form of local government is that the insulation from politics enables the city manager to more effectively pursue the politically unpopular, but administratively necessary, decisions. Given this rationale, should Grant Albert even consider the political ramifications of his decision in this matter?
2. What are the advantages to the city of proceeding with the termination of Deputy City Manager Tom Gilchrist? What are the disadvantages?
3. What are the ethical issues arising from Gilchrist's actions on the Fourth of July?
4. What are the implications for Albert's authority if he reinstates Gilchrist?
5. What are the possible major consequences for Albert as city manager if he stands by his original decision to terminate Gilchrist?
6. What are the foreseeable benefits and problems in Albert's compromising his decision on what to do about Gilchrist?
7. Was termination warranted, based on Tom Gilchrist's actions?
8. Many public organizations have a progressive discipline process with sequential steps that must be followed prior to termination. The city of Lakeview does not have such guidelines. Should Lakeview consider implementing a progressive discipline process for all public employees? Is such a process appropriate or ideal for the highest ranking administrators? How might this affect the city manager's ability to make important personnel decisions?
9. What type of employee monitoring systems could Lakeview consider to avoid situations like this in the future? Should strict employee monitoring guidelines be implemented specifically for the city manager's office?
10. What should Grant Albert do? Why?

Suggested Simulation Roles

Grant Albert, city manager
Tom Gilchrist, deputy city manager
Sharon Collins, mayor
City council members
Citizens
Witnesses to the events of the Fourth of July
Civil Service Review Board Members

Part II

Achieving Effective Community Leadership

Introduction to Part II

Achieving Effective Community Leadership

Jurisdictions vary greatly. They grow (or shrink) in population at different rates. They have highly varied industrial and commercial bases. Some have only upscale housing; others have economically diverse neighborhoods. Some communities have almost no ethnic diversity; others have a rich blend of ethnic and national heritages.

Communities also vary as to their needs. Some adamantly adhere to the status quo and want only caretaker governance. Others seek modest growth and development. Still others demand a change agent because their goal is to transform themselves into something quite different.

The effective manager must size up the characteristics of the community and the kind of leadership that the council and the public are seeking. Otherwise, the manager is perennially out of step with the community and in danger of early departure. Moreover, the manager cannot live up to his or her professional obligation to help the governing body develop appropriate public policies. Often the manager must play the role of mediator, trying to reconcile two or more sharply contrasting views.

Cases 4, 5, and 6 in Part II describe managers' attempts to provide effective leadership to the community, but in significantly different circumstances and with varying degrees of success. In Case 4, "The Fire File," the manager must solve the problem of providing adequate firefighting services, a function that all communities must address. However, a strong union, fiscal stress, political rancor, and insubordination complicate the problem. Can the manager find a solution acceptable to most of the players?

"Town and Gown," Case 5, focuses on a not atypical history of poor relations between a municipality and a local university. Long-simmering disagreements come to the fore when a piece of property becomes available outside the university's traditional boundaries. The university intends to put the property to a "higher and best use" than any other likely purchaser, but will the neighborhood accept the school's encroachment? Is there a way to bring town and gown together?

Case 6, "Theft in an Elective Office," concerns shortfalls in city accounts, electoral politics, and official misconduct. Can the administrator "make the problems go away," or will the scandal cripple the city? The case includes elements of financial (mis)management and human resource management (employee turnover) as well as "bad press."

Cases in Part II emphasize a number of management practices: staff effectiveness, policy facilitation, functional and operational expertise, citizen service, initiative and risk taking, citizenship participation, financial and human resource management, media relations, and integrity. Collectively, they offer something for everyone.

4

The Fire File

Scott D. Lazenby

Background

Trillium is a suburban city of 45,000 residents within a metropolitan area in the Pacific Northwest. At the time the case unfolds, an initiative by the city's voters has precipitated a serious budget crisis, forcing the city government's officials to consider major changes in the way it serves (or discontinues serving) its citizens.

The case is based on the author's novel *Playing with Fire* (New York: Writers Club Press, 2001). The cast of characters is as follows:

Ben Cromarty, City Manager

Betty Sue Castle, Assistant City Manager

Ken Longstreet, Finance Director

Max Oakley, Fire Chief

Diane McTavish, Mayor

Rob Titus, Maggie Henderson, Seth Rosenberg, Hank Arnold, City Council Members

Todd Pritchard, Business Owner

The Case

Clipping file, *The Oregonian,* May 25

TRILLIUM VOTERS PUT THE SQUEEZE ON CITY TAXES

TRILLIUM–With 85% of the precincts reporting, it appears that Trillium voters have dealt their city government a serious blow in Tuesday's special election. Measure 3-47, approved by a 72% majority, rolls back the property tax paid by any individual property to its level of five years ago. Estimates of the measure's impact on city revenues range from a reduction of 15% to 25%. Trillium business owner Todd Pritchard, author of the measure, celebrated the victory with other business owners Tuesday night at the Plow & Harrow Pub. "We don't have anything against the city; we just think they need to live within their means, like all us businesses do," Pritchard said. City Manager Ben Cromarty said that although city officials were surprised by the outcome of the election, they were committed to carrying out the will of the voters.

CITY OF TRILLIUM
MEMORANDUM

DATE: June 17
TO: Department Heads
FROM: Ben Cromarty, City Manager
SUBJECT: Budget Decision Packages in Response to Measure 3-47

As we discussed during our staff meeting, the City Council would like to see decision packages for budget reductions that add up to at least 30% of each department's net budget. At their retreat, the Council members emphasized that they are open to new ways of providing services, and anything that could result in a major reduction in expenses is open for discussion. They also provided direction that we not attempt to punish the voters for their decision, and that we avoid putting out sacred cows for cuts (although, I suppose, one person's sacred cow is another person's steak dinner). Bottom line—no game playing.

Please submit your decision packages to Ken Longstreet by **August 20.** If you want to run any ideas by me before then, please feel free.

ELECTRONIC MAIL

INBOX FOR USERNAME BCROMARTY
FROM: BSCASTLE
POSTED: JULY 8/7:50:01AM
SUBJECT: Budget Idea

Ben,

You said to leave no stone unturned, so I'm taking your word for it. I have an idea for restructuring fire and EMS services that can potentially save a huge amount of money. Interested? Terri said you have an opening at 3 tomorrow. Could we talk about it?

—Betty Sue

ELECTRONIC MAIL

INBOX FOR USERNAME BSCASTLE
FROM: BCROMARTY
POSTED: JULY 8/5:20:22PM
SUBJECT: Re: Budget Idea

Betty Sue,

No problem (3 p.m. tomorrow is OK). You haven't talked to Chief Oakley about this, have you? I know the Council said they were interested in innovation, but I doubt that includes tinkering with the fire department. Anyway, catch you tomorrow.

—BC

ANALYSIS OF EFFICIENCIES IN THE PROVISION OF FIRE AND EMERGENCY MEDICAL SERVICES

Submitted July 15
to Ben Cromarty, City Manager
by Betty Sue Castle, Assistant City Manager
and Ken Longstreet, Finance Director

Historically, fire departments entered the EMS business because their firefighters were trained in first aid, they were set up to respond to calls quickly, and fire calls left plenty of time to respond to medical calls. But now, the Trillium Fire Department, like many other departments, spends most of its time responding to EMS calls, and not fire calls. They have, in effect, become primarily an EMS department and only secondarily a fire department. But they are organized and operated as if their primary mission has never changed. Is this the most efficient way to provide the service? Twenty-four-hour shifts, three-person crews, and a fleet of $600,000 pumpers make sense if what you are mostly doing is putting out fires, but is this the best configuration for responding to medical calls?

Response time is critical for some medical emergencies such as strokes and heart attacks. But it has become less critical for building fires: smoke alarms save the people in the building, and delays in reporting the fire have a bigger effect on property loss than the travel time by the fire trucks. Using this information, we have explored a scenario in which *staff and operations are specifically and separately targeted to fire and EMS responses.*

EXISTING SITUATION

Station One has two three-firefighter crews, and each of the other two stations has a single crew. The firefighters work twenty-four-hour shifts and are off forty-eight hours, so there are three shifts, each with its own battalion chief. That adds up to thirty-six firefighters and three battalion chiefs. Each shift also has two spare firefighters, to fill in for vacations and other absences, bringing the total up to forty-two. Using the current averages for salaries, overtime, and fringe benefits, the annual cost is $4.8 million.

Each station has a pumper, and Station Two has a smaller rescue rig. Station One has a ladder truck. To operate all this equipment, we spend around $500,000 a year on fuel, parts, insurance, and so on. The trucks themselves are paid through General Obligation bonds, so the capital cost doesn't directly affect the operating budget. Uniforms, tools, repairs, training, and so on account for another $100,000. In total, the cost to operate the department is around $5.4 million per year. This does not include the department's management costs—captains, assistant chiefs, fire marshal, fire inspection and prevention, public information officer, and so on. (See the current budget for the fire department at the end of this memo.)

ALTERNATIVE SERVICE DELIVERY

Based on actual calls for service, we believe that for medical calls, we could easily get by with four two-person crews during the day shift and swing shift, and three crews during the graveyard shift. In making these projections, we used queuing theory to take into account the fact that the calls don't spread themselves evenly through the day, but instead come in bunches. These crews would work eight-hour shifts. Based on the experience of other cities that operate ambulance companies, it costs $110 per hour to operate an ambulance with a two-person crew. We would face start-up costs of purchasing ambulances, but this could be offset by selling surplus fire apparatus. We have enough fire fighters with EMS training to provide this service in house, but we could

(continued)

?

also contract out for it. This might be an option if the negotiating with the firefighters union becomes too problematic.

For actual fires, 95 percent of our nonmedical fire calls could be handled by a three-person crew operating out of Station One. Staff costs would be $1.1 million, and operating costs another $125,000. For larger fires, we could contract with neighboring cities on a per-fire basis. Based on past experience, there would less than one per year. Other staff could also be trained as volunteer firefighters. In fact, it is easier to recruit volunteers if they don't face the constant grind of medical calls.

NET SAVINGS

Overall, reconfiguring our fire and medical operations this way could save over $600,000 per year. It could also provide better service: we now have the capability to respond simultaneously to four medical and fire calls; the proposed configuration would allow us to respond to five simultaneous calls during the busier day and swing shifts. The ambulance companies would be mobile and could be based to provide the lowest overall response time to calls. This is more difficult with fire companies based at fire stations, which tend to be fairly permanent and difficult to move.

CURRENT BUDGET SUMMARY
TRILLIUM FIRE DEPARTMENT

	Current Budget
Administration	
Salary & Fringe Benefits	$360,766
Supplies & Services	$68,000
Equipment	$26,000
Support Services (Prevention, Training, PIO)	
Salary & Fringe Benefits	$143,799
Supplies & Services	$56,000
Equipment	$15,000
Operations—Fire & EMS	
Salary & Fringe Benefits	$4,796,533
Supplies & Services	$608,588
Equipment	$173,000
TOTAL	$6,247,686

ELECTRONIC MAIL

INBOX FOR USERNAME BCROMARTY
FROM: MOAKLEY
POSTED: JULY 17/3:23:33 PM
SUBJECT: Meddling with Fire

Ben,

While Longstreet and Castle briefed me on their "little proposal," I remain unconvinced. The situation is not as simple as they seem to think. Many of our calls require a fire *and* medical response. A good percentage of our medical calls are related to vehicle accidents, where there is typically a danger of fire due to gasoline and other combustibles. Conversely, many structure fires have a potential for injury, not only to the public but to our own personnel.
In any case, I do not appreciate a kid five years out of college presuming that she knows how to operate a public safety department. I think you will find that a radical restructuring of the fire service is unacceptable.

–Chief Max Oakley

Clipping file, *The Oregonian,* July 25

TRILLIUM FIREFIGHTERS UNION OUTRAGED

TRILLIUM–Reacting to an internal memo proposing to shave costs in the fire department, the Trillium Firefighters Association issued a press release warning of imminent danger to life and property. "Trillium residents are rightly concerned with any proposal to shut down two of our three fire stations," said Union President Brian Gallagher. "We won't stand by and see our citizens put at risk like that."

The proposal, prepared by Assistant City Manager Betty Sue Castle and Finance Director Ken Longstreet, recommends using two-person ambulance crews to respond to emergency medical calls, rather than the current three-person firefighter crews. Only one of the three fire stations would be staffed to respond to fire calls. "No decisions have been made; this is just one of many options we're looking at as a way to continue to provide services in the wake of Measure 3-47," said City Manager Ben Cromarty.

The Trillium City Council has not yet reviewed the budget options, according to Mayor Diane McTavish. "Ben (Cromarty) briefed us individually on the alternatives under consideration, but we haven't received any formal recommendations," McTavish said. Council member Rob Titus stated that he supports the firefighters. "This is just another case where the city manager has blind-sided the Council," he said.

Correspondence files

OREGON AMBULANCE SERVICE

23122 Main Street
Tigard, OR 97223
Mr. Ben Cromarty, City Manager

August 6
City of Trillium
39250 Skoomkumchuk Drive
Trillium, OR 97035

Dear Mr. Cromarty:

Thank you for your interest in contracting with Oregon Ambulance for the provision of emergency medical services for the citizens of Trillium. We do believe we could provide the service very effectively and efficiently.

Our corporate management team has considered this request very carefully. At this point, however, we must decline to submit a proposal. While we realize that you are seeking the most cost-effective way to serve your residents, some may see a proposal from OAS as merely a bargaining chip in the current conflict between the City and the fire union. Our employees interact with members of the International Brotherhood of Firefighters on a daily basis, and we do not wish to do anything that might strain that relationship.

You have asked for general cost information for planning purposes. We can confirm that a number of around $100 per hour for basic EMS service is a good figure; we are able to stay under that amount in communities where we do provide first-response service.

Sincerely,

Joe Secomb, NW Regional Vice President

cc: Betty Sue Castle, Assistant City Manager
Brian Gallagher, President, Trillium Firefighters Local 255

ELECTRONIC MAIL

INBOX FOR USERNAME BCROMARTY
FROM: BSCASTLE
POSTED: AUGUST 13/5:23:02 PM
SUBJECT: Contract EMS Alternative

Ben, since OAS wimped out on us, I went ahead and contacted City/County Fire Services out of Glendale, AZ. They provide private fire and EMS service for a lot of the southwest cities, and said they would be very interested in getting a toehold in the NW. Should I try to get a proposal from them?

INBOX FOR USERNAME BSCASTLE
FROM: BCROMARTY
POSTED: AUGUST 14/2:12:56 PM
SUBJECT: Re: Contract EMS Alternative

Betty Sue,

Had lunch today with Matt Monroe of City/County Fire. He said they could provide EMS service for $90 per hour if they also got the franchise for the ambulance transport to the hospitals–said they can often bill insurance for the transport and help keep our cost down. He'll get us a draft proposal next week.

–Ben

INBOX FOR USERNAME BCROMARTY
FROM: BSCASTLE
POSTED: AUGUST 14/2:14:06 PM
SUBJECT: Re: Re: Contract EMS Alternative

Sounds good. It would have been nice if you had included me in the meeting.

–Betty Sue

INBOX FOR USERNAME BSCASTLE
FROM: BCROMARTY
POSTED: AUGUST 14/2:22:56 PM
SUBJECT: Re: Re: Re: Contract EMS Alternative

Betty Sue,

You're right–sorry.

–Ben

Trillium City Council

Official Minutes
Regular Meeting
September 4

New Business

Proposal from City/County Fire Services to Provide Emergency Medical Services

City Manager Ben Cromarty summarized the proposal from City/County Fire Services to provide contracted EMS service to the City. He stated that by privatizing the service, costs would be lower. The draft contract includes response times and service quality guarantees to ensure the company doesn't take short cuts. A key provision of the draft agreement is that City/County would offer positions to any Trillium Fire Department employees who might be laid off due to the reconfiguration of service. At this stage, it is only a proposal for consideration, but staff needs direction from the Council before proceeding.

(continued)

Mayor McTavish called for public comment. Matt Monroe, City/County Fire Services, said his business has a solid track record of providing service for communities. Firefighter Brian Gallagher stated he was representing the fire union, and that in his eighteen years of service, he had never seen such an irresponsible action by city management. Todd Pritchard of the Trillium Business Leadership Committee said the businessmen of the community supported their fire department and the first priority of the city should be to cut waste and unnecessary spending, not to meddle with critical services. Kate Anderson with the Trillium Print Shop said that Mr. Pritchard did not speak for all business owners, and that decisions on reorganizing to cut costs aren't always easy, but they often make good business sense.

Mayor McTavish then called for Council discussion. Council member Seth Rosenberg said that he was concerned about the treatment of the city employees, especially the firefighters, but City/County's offer to hire the employees went a long way to addressing his concern. As far as critical services go, the city would still respond to fire calls, and medical services have a tradition of being provided by the private sector in America. He said the Council should consider it carefully. Council Member Maggie Henderson said she was concerned that no city had tried it. Mayor McTavish responded that many cities in the Southwest had used City/County for years. Councillor Henderson said she still had concerns. Council Member Rob Titus asked Chief Oakley to comment on the proposal. Oakley replied that he believed contracting would be a bad idea and would put citizens in danger. Titus then said that for a decision this important, the people should vote on it. Mayor McTavish pointed out that the people elected the Council to make difficult decisions like this.

Motion: Direct staff to bring a formal contract with City/County Fire Services for consideration at the next meeting.
Moved by: Councillor Rosenberg
Seconded by: Councillor Arnold

The motion passed by a 3-to-2 vote, with Councillors Henderson and Titus opposing the motion.

Clipping file, *The Oregonian*, September 15

TURBULENT TIMES IN TRILLIUM

TRILLIUM—Todd Pritchard, Trillium business owner and president of the Trillium Business Leadership Committee, announced a drive by his organization to recall three members of the Trillium city council. By casting votes in favor of a private contract for emergency medical services, Mayor Diane McTavish and council members Seth Rosenberg and Hank Arnold demonstrated they are "out of touch with the community," according to Pritchard. "Their actions reflect an overall inability to reflect the will of the people," Pritchard said in a prepared statement.

McTavish said she was unimpressed with the business committee's action. "Todd Pritchard is just a pipsqueak—thinks he's running a government in exile," she commented when approached at her usual booth in the Fir Away Café.

In a related action, the business committee on September 12 held a call-in vote on whether City Manager Ben Cromarty should be fired. The informal poll, conducted by Pritchard and his business colleagues on Trillium Cable Access Channel 97, showed that 57% of the program's viewers supported Cromarty's resignation. Council member Rob Titus stated that he is becoming concerned about the reliability of the advice that the council is receiving from the city manager and that the straw poll clearly shows the staff is out of touch with the people.

CITY OF TRILLIUM
MEMORANDUM

DATE: September 22
TO: Ben Cromarty
FROM: Max Oakley, Fire Chief
SUBJECT: Potential Merger with River Valley Fire District

I have been approached by River Valley Fire about the possibility of annexing the City of Trillium into their district. Our existing department would be merged into theirs, and the city would be relieved of the financial burden of the entire fire department.

As you know, River Valley began as a fairly small rural fire district, but over time, many of the suburban cities have annexed to the district or contracted for services. Their district also includes a large amount of commercial and industrial areas in the unincorporated urban area, which adds to the tax base without placing a major burden on services.

If Trillium voters approve annexation to the district, our employees would be transferred straight across, taking with them their seniority and accrued vacation and sick leave. They would be moved to higher pay ranges, with more promotion opportunities. Our firefighters are very supportive of this option, and Brian Gallagher has informed me that the Firefighters Brotherhood would provide major funding for an election campaign.

Trillium property owners would have to pay taxes to the district, but their tax rate is only $2.50 per $1,000 in assessed value, which is very reasonable for a high level of both fire and EMS response. But by moving the cost of fire and EMS services to the district, it would save the city's general fund $6.2 million a year, which would solve your budget problem while avoiding a major fight with the union. (I have been informed that the firefighters organized the response to the call-in program that called for your resignation.)

I have attached a copy of the ballot initiative that the City of Springdale used when they annexed to the district, for your information. I can have a Resolution for a similar ballot measure for us prepared for the next Council agenda.

Sample ballot used for the City of Springdale when it annexed to the district – MO

RIVER VALLEY FIRE DISTRICT
MEASURE 3-302

Ballot Title
ANNEXATION OF SPRINGDALE AREA TO THE RIVER VALLEY FIRE DISTRICT

QUESTION: Shall territory within the City of Springdale city limits be annexed to the River Valley Fire District?

☐ Yes

☐ No

SUMMARY: If approved, this measure would allow voters in the City of Springdale to annex into the River Valley Fire District. If voters permit annexation into the District, newly annexed areas would pay the District property tax rate, currently $2.50 per $1,000 of assessed value. This measure would expand the territory of the district for both services and revenue collection. The River Valley Fire District is a special district organized under provisions of state law, and it is governed by a five-member Board of Directors elected at large by residents within the district.

INBOX FOR USERNAME MOAKLEY
FROM: BCROMARTY
POSTED: SEPTEMBER 23/7:22:06 AM
SUBJECT: River Valley Fire District

Max,

Hold off on any further discussions with River Valley Fire. As a resident and taxpayer myself, I think annexing to the district would be an absolute rip-off–each homeowner would be paying around $600 a year more in property tax without much of an increase in the level of service they get. We would lose local control too. The district serves over a half million residents, yet no one has a clue who the board members are.

–Ben

WHILE YOU WERE OUT
PHONE MESSAGE

Date: 9/25
Time: 2:30 p.m.
For: Ben
From: (Anonymous–said he was a retired employee, but wouldn't give his name)

Message: Called to let you know he overheard Max Oakley and Rob Titus having a discussion in a booth at the Fir Away Café. Said that Max accused you of blocking an idea of his, and it sounded like he was trying to go over your head. Just thought you should know.

–Terri

The Decision Problem

Ben Cromarty believes that privatizing emergency medical service and scaling back fire service makes the most sense in terms of government efficiency. Yet his initial instinct to avoid crossing swords with the fire union has proved to be valid. Is the potential savings really worth the continuing personal and organizational conflict? And now it appears that Max Oakley has made an end run to a council member with the proposal to annex to the large fire district.

If you were in the city manager's position, what would you do? What would you recommend to the council, and what would you do with the proposal to annex to the fire district? How would you handle your renegade department head, Max Oakley?

Discussion Questions

1. Was City Manager Ben Cromarty too quick to dismiss Fire Chief Max Oakley's proposal to annex into the River Valley Fire District? What other options could the city have considered in reducing costs (or increasing revenues) in the fire department?
2. Max Oakley is not a team player, and his interactions with the city manager seem to verge on insubordination. Yet he has cultivated a relationship with at

least one city council member. How should Cromarty deal with this situation? Should Cromarty have attempted to make Oakley a part of the initial decision team?

3. Backlash from the firefighters union prompted Ben Cromarty and Assistant City Manager Betty Sue Castle to explore privatizing part of the service rather than simply reorganizing the organization. As city manager, what steps could you take to try to get buy-in from the union at the outset?
4. How far should Cromarty go in selling a solution to the general public?
5. Council Member Rob Titus evidences a certain amount of animosity toward Ben Cromarty. How could the city manager attempt to improve the relationship? What if Titus is motivated by the media attention resulting from his attacks on the staff?
6. At their September 4 council meeting, the decision makers had a lot of opinions available. Did they have adequate information to make a choice? If not, what additional information should Cromarty have given them?
7. What information should be provided to council for future decisions on this issue?

Suggested Simulation Roles

Assign one group of students the management role (city manager, assistant city manager, and finance director) and another group the firefighters union role (local president, union representative, and professional negotiator from the International Brotherhood of Firefighters). The task of the management team is to come up with strategies to gain the cooperation of the union in a restructuring of the fire department, along the lines first proposed by Assistant City Manager Betty Sue Castle and Finance Director Ken Longstreet.

The union team is open to any ideas that improve the conditions and compensation of the firefighters *as long as* 24-hour shifts with three-firefighter crews are maintained. In fact, the brotherhood is putting strong pressure on the local union to insist on four-firefighter crews.

Let the teams play through several scenarios and strategies. Do any of them seem to work?

Add more interest by assigning a group of rank-and-file firefighters who are not active in the union but are nevertheless committed to the firefighting profession, as well as a group of concerned citizens. Encourage the primary teams (management and union) to come up with creative ways to involve these groups in their strategies.

5

Town and Gown

Carmine Scavo

Background

A Southeastern city of about 75,000 houses a large and fast-growing state university. The university is located near the downtown area and is surrounded by older neighborhoods. Much of the growth in the city has taken place on its outskirts, away from the university. The university student population has grown from 12,000 to 25,000 in a little over twenty years. The neighborhoods surrounding the university have experienced a great deal of change, from almost exclusively single-family, owner-occupied housing to multiple-unit housing. Housing prices in the city have increased faster than the national average, with a recent spike in prices occurring in the early 2000s.

The neighborhood north of the university had long been one of combined owner–occupants and renters. The owner–occupants were both university faculty, who preferred to live close to work, and older residents of the city, who liked living where their families had traditionally lived. As this second group of residents aged, they often sold their homes to investors who divided them up into apartments and rented them to university students. Many of the houses in the neighborhood dated from a time when the city taxed housing on the basis of its linear footage on the street; omitting the space for a driveway thus meant lower property taxes.

This taxation practice also meant that neighborhood residents viewed on-street parking spaces in front of their privately owned homes as *their* spaces rather than public parking—the way the police and city officials viewed such spots. Because some of these properties were rented by students with cars, conflict between owner–occupants and renters increased and "the university" was widely blamed for the problem. This conflict involved not only parking but also late-night party noise, lack of upkeep in rental properties, and general lifestyle issues.

The university's reputation in the neighborhood also suffered from some development decisions the university had made over time. North Street—a two-lane, tree-lined street—was the historic boundary between the university on the south and the neighborhood to the north, but, over time, the university had managed to buy several of the older homes on the north side of North Street for use as university offices. Several fraternities and sororities also purchased and rehabilitated large old homes on the north side of North Street.

Neighborhood activists wanted to maintain the owner-occupied nature of the neighborhood. They wanted no new multifamily development. What they did want was reduced on-street parking for nonresidents, increased use of "traffic calming" (speed bumps, four-way stop signs, and the like), and the prevention of further university expansion into the neighborhood. Their plan had three elements. They wanted (1) to negotiate with the university; (2) to lobby the city directly for new regulations on noise, parking, maximum number of unrelated occupants in rental units, and related matters; and (3) to pursue National Historic Registry designation to curtail university expansion.

The administration had resisted inclusion of the university in the proposed historic district even though many of the older university buildings on campus would certainly qualify for such status. The university's reluctance on this point, coupled with growing conflicts over parking and development, further soured neighborhood-university relations, resulting in several awkward meetings between neighborhood activists and university officials. The chancellor's statement at one public meeting—that "the university was in the business of education, not environmental management, preservation, or other social concerns"—caused neighborhood activists even more consternation. In addition, the university began a long-term, expansionary effort and circulated plans that would require more land for academic buildings and dormitories. More students would mean more demand for parking, but parking lots were missing from the university plan.

The situation came to a head over a North Street house being considered for historic status. After buying the house, the university announced that it would raze it to make way for a visitors' parking lot. Neighborhood activists protested the university's plan and demanded to meet with university officials to negotiate the fate of the house. Eventually, the vice chancellor for business affairs scheduled the requested meeting, where the following discussion took place.

Vice chancellor for business affairs: I am glad we could all get together to discuss this. Would anybody like coffee?

Head of the neighborhood association: We really don't want the old house to be torn down—especially to make way for a parking lot. That house has historic significance. We want to preserve it as an example of what this neighborhood was and wants to be again.

Vice chancellor for business affairs (glancing at his watch): Well, I'm sorry that you feel this way but at this very moment bulldozers are razing the house. The parking lot will be completed in several weeks.

Neighborhood activists: What? How could you do this? Why did we even have this meeting if you already knew that the demolition had been scheduled?

Vice chancellor for business affairs: May I ask how many of you work for the university? I would suspect it is a fairly large number. Doesn't your livelihood depend on a healthy and growing university? What would happen if the university couldn't grow? We would have to downsize staff, and some of your jobs might be vulnerable.

Neighborhood activists: Is that a threat?

Vice chancellor for business affairs: No, it isn't a threat—it is simply a fact of life. Growth is difficult—it demands tradeoffs, and the sacrifice of this one building means the health of the entire university and the preservation of a number of jobs. National historic designation is a pipe dream—the university will never agree to come under neighborhood historic district guidelines. Don't you understand that?

Head of the neighborhood association: Oh, so you want to play hardball?

The meeting ended in confusion. The head of the neighborhood association convened a meeting of neighborhood activists, and they immediately began to make plans. First, they moved to request changes in the zoning in their neighborhood. The existing zoning was predominantly residential. This designation restricted commercial use but allowed institutional housing—fraternity and sorority houses, boarding houses, private dormitories, and so forth—only as preexisting, nonconforming uses. The wife of the chair of the neighborhood group, who was herself a city council member, introduced changes to neighborhood zoning. Eventually they were adopted, resulting in the most restrictive zoning in the city. The new zoning designation basically forbade institutional use in the entire neighborhood. This change meant that, while the university could own property in the neighborhood, it could not use it for offices, dormitories, or any other university-related purpose.

The university's response to this ordinance was to seek an opinion from the state attorney general on whether state agencies (such as public universities) were bound by local zoning codes. The attorney general's office agreed to consider the issue. However, the attorney general, knowing the contentiousness of the issue and realizing the decision would affect not only this one university but also university–town relations for all member institutions in the state university system, delayed issuing the opinion and required a detailed study.

Meanwhile, neighborhood activists lobbied for stricter enforcement of a city ordinance prohibiting more than three unrelated individuals to share a dwelling unless that dwelling had already been deemed a rooming house. Rooming houses were allowed only in certain zones within the city. (Fraternity and sorority houses were formally rooming houses, according to the city zoning code, and were allowed in this neighborhood only as "nonconforming uses.") These activists also sponsored legislation creating a neighborhood parking plan by which residents might park on neighborhood streets for unlimited amounts of time, whereas other vehicles could park for only two hours.

Buoyed by early successes in their quest for neighborhood preservation, neighborhood activists were optimistic. Time brought changes in both the university and city administrations although the roster of neighborhood activists remained essentially unchanged. The new university administration emphasized improving relations with surrounding neighborhoods, and the newly hired city manager also sought better relations between city residents and the university. The city manager had come from a different city within the same state. This was his first appointment as a city manager, but he had extensive experience as an assistant manager in both smaller and larger cities. The new university chancellor had come from a different state; thus, both he and the city manager were largely ignorant of the bad blood stemming from previous interactions of the university, the city, and the neighborhood.

At the start of his new job, the city manager made an appointment to meet with the university chancellor. At that meeting the city manager proposed establishing an informal group of city, university, and neighborhood stakeholders who would have lunch together and address common problems. The university chancellor's assistant—a longtime university faculty member and one-time neighborhood resident—was appointed as the contact person for neighborhood affairs. Led by the city manager, these discussions initially involved the city manager's office, neighborhood groups, and commercial interests in the university area. The meetings typically were positive in tone, and neighborhood activists began to see progress in improving relations with the university.

The weekly luncheons, soon known as the "Town and Gown Committee," addressed several thorny issues. One of the committee's first actions was to address the large and raucous Halloween celebration downtown. A tradition of sorts, the Halloween event attracted as many as 10,000 people coming into the city for a street party that was the largest of its type in the state.

In this first year of the Town and Gown Committee, Halloween fell on a Saturday, with a university home football game scheduled earlier in the day. The city police chief had expressed concern about the number of people—students, alumni, "outsiders," and others—who would be downtown for Halloween and the ability of his police force to control such a large crowd.

The Town and Gown Committee successfully met this concern in three ways: by increasing coordination between the city and university police departments; by encouraging alternate events at the university; and by demanding that downtown club owners help enforce city and state regulations on underage drinking and public consumption of alcohol.

The city manager was pleased with his role in the increased cooperation between the city, university, downtown business interests, and the neighborhood. He looked forward to further conciliation and a common approach to solving future problems. However, he also realized that the cooperation was mostly ad hoc in nature, dependent on his carefully nurtured personal relationships with university administrators, downtown business owners, neighborhood activists, and city officials. He knew this cooperative spirit could be derailed by any single action that implied his acting in bad faith.

The Case

At about this time, the out-of-town owner of a small office building two blocks north of the university decided to sell it. The building was part of a two-unit development that originally was the first home of the county hospital. One of the two buildings had been rehabilitated into offices; the other sat vacant. When the university approached the owner about selling the building, he agreed. The university wanted to use the building for its institutional development office—the fundraising arm of the university.

The sale of the building was suddenly in jeopardy when the university attorney learned of the neighborhood's changed zoning status: the university could not operate the building as an office unless it was approved for nonconforming use. The chancellor's assistant advised the university administration that if neighborhood activists opposed it, the city planning department and city council would not support nonconforming use status. The university's purchase of the building was thus predicated on neighborhood approval.

In the years since its first confrontation with the university, the neighborhood activists' group had formalized its structure. It now had a nine-person, elected executive board that met weekly and a dues-paying membership of several hundred people who met monthly. When the university first approached the neighborhood association about purchasing the building, several members of the executive board cited the history of neighborhood interactions with the university, including how the neighborhood thought it repeatedly had been "taken" by the university. Other board members differed, contending that the university could be a good neighbor and most likely would maintain the property better than a private owner.

Other neighborhood concerns persisted, a key one being that the building's parking lot was too large for the institutional advancement staff's cars; therefore, the university might be tempted to use the lot to store other university vehicles such as vans and trucks. Because staff in institutional advancement worked late into the evening, a second concern was commotion and traffic at night. Last, lingering in the background was the symbolic issue of university ownership in the neighborhood.

The city manager saw no good remedies if neighborhood residents opposed any university operation of the site due to the new zoning, even as he saw the advantages of university ownership and operation of the building—especially since the building had been vacant for a year. He worried that a confrontation between the university and the neighborhood would irreparably damage the fragile peace he had facilitated. Moreover, he worried that the university could go back to the state attorney general asking for an opinion that state institutions were immune from the provisions of city zoning codes. This would leave the city with little say in any expansion by the university.

The city manager saw three options:

1. To side with the university and support its ownership of the property, knowing that this approach violated the zoning code but also knowing that the property would be well maintained;
2. To side with the neighborhood and support the zoning code, knowing that the property might remain vacant and that the university possibly could get a ruling from the state attorney general to the effect that it was immune from local zoning code provisions; or
3. To pursue agreement between the two parties using the Town and Gown Committee format.

The manager decided to bring the issue to the Town and Gown Committee. Word of the possible exception to the neighborhood zoning plan reached the ears of the city's planning director just hours before the committee was to meet. Having been with the city for some fifteen years, the planning director was familiar with the history of the university-neighborhood interaction. He did not live in the affected neighborhood; in fact he lived fairly far from the university and had no personal stake in any proposed solution. Under his direction, the city planning department had been working on cleaning up the city's zoning map for a long time. The map he inherited from the previous director showed a large amount of "shotgun zoning"—small parcels of land (even individual buildings) zoned differently from the surrounding zone. These zoning decisions were often made as a result of individual petitions, and the planning director thought they signified political pressure on the city.

The planning director did not know whether he would be asked to speak at the Town and Gown Committee meeting or what he should say if the city manager asked him to speak about the proposed nonconforming use for the office building. His notion of professionalism was in conflict with his sense of self-protection. Opposing the city manager in public was not a good career move for him, yet he did not want to be pressured into agreeing to an unjustified zone change.

As the planning director saw it, his choices were:

1. To agree with the variance at the meeting, knowing that the nonconforming use went against his professional notions of comprehensive zoning but maintained his good relations with the city manager;
2. To disagree with the city manager at the meeting, knowing it would be consistent with his professional norms but also might cost him his job—or at least his good standing with the manager; or
3. To miss the meeting because of illness or for some other reason.

City manager: You all know why we are here. The university has proposed buying the property on Third and Elm streets. The zoning in the neighborhood does not support this kind of use. The only way that the university can use the property as it wishes is to receive a nonconforming use exemption. I would not support such an exemption unless you support it unanimously. What do you all think about this?

Chair of neighborhood association: There are good reasons why we would support an exemption, but there are also good reasons why we would oppose it. I think that we should just open the floor up to a general discussion and allow everybody to have a say on this. Who's first?

Old-time neighborhood resident: I will never support an exemption—it would violate the longtime verbal agreement that the university will never jump North Street.

Second neighborhood resident: But the university already owns property on the north side of North Street. How can you say that you would never support its ownership of this property when it was your family that sold them the house on North Street that is now the university alumni office?

Old-time neighborhood resident: That house is on North Street—that's not the same thing as jumping North Street!

Third neighborhood resident: The university really has been a good neighbor. They do a good job of keeping up the appearance of university owned buildings—they are clean, the grass is mowed, the buildings are in good repair. The shrubbery and trees on the south side of North Street are an excellent example of university stewardship. And remember, they took over care of the old oak trees on the street when the city was having financial problems. The city would have let those trees die.

Fourth neighborhood resident: University ownership and operation of the building is much better than either the building remaining vacant—especially since it already has several broken windows—or having a private owner who might not maintain it very well. The last thing I want to see is that building turning into something trashy. That would be a blight on this entire neighborhood.

Neighborhood resident who lives next to the site: What about traffic? What about comings and goings at night? What about trucks and vans being stored in the large parking lot? These are my concerns since I live right next door.

Chancellor's assistant: I have several things I'd like to clear up. First, no university vehicles other than those used by institutional advancement staff would be allowed to park in the building parking lot. Second, no overnight parking by any university vehicles would be allowed. Third, nighttime activities in the building would be as low-key as possible—no all-night outside lights on. And fourth, the university will redo the plantings around the building to make it more attractive.

Chair of the neighborhood association: What about the historic district?

Chancellor's assistant: We are reconsidering our opposition to participating in the proposed historic district. I can't guarantee that we will go along with the plan for the historic district, but we won't oppose it.

Chair of the neighborhood association: Do the residents have any more questions or comments?

Old-time neighborhood resident: I guess I could support university ownership if all these things that they are saying are really true. But I don't want this exception to set any precedent or any-

(continued)

thing. Just because we are agreeing to this deal doesn't mean that the university has a free hand in buying up property throughout this neighborhood. We've been taken by the university before, and I sure hope we don't get taken again.

City manager: I assure you that this will not set a precedent. Remember, this proposal is for nonconforming use, meaning that this individual property does not conform to the general zoning of the neighborhood. The city code says that all nonconforming uses must be agreed to by property owners in surrounding properties. Here we have not only the property owners but also residents of the entire neighborhood. This is the kind of cooperative planning that this city really needs. I see this as the wave of the future. To keep our momentum, let's go around the room, identifying ourselves by name and affiliation and stating whether or not we endorse university purchase of the property. As I stated at the beginning, I will support the nonconforming use of the building only if everybody in the room agrees to it.

Neighborhood activists, city planning staff, representatives of the university, and residents who lived in the vicinity of the affected property—some 25 individuals in all—attended the meeting. The city manager convened the meeting.

Everyone then spoke in turn about the issue, affirming that he or she thought the nonconforming use was personally acceptable and speaking in favor of university ownership. One of the last to comment was the planning director.

City planning director: The planning department is opposed to the nonconforming use in this case. The department has spent the last fifteen years attempting to reduce the amount of shotgun zoning in this city. Here we have an example of everything we have fought against. The zoning for this neighborhood was changed just a few years ago. The process included study by the planning department, followed by consideration and agreement by the planning board and then by the city council. All in all, it took almost three months for the process to play itself out. Now, in just one short hour, all of this work is about to be undone as we let the university operate an office in a zone that does not allow such use.

City manager: Seeing as all neighborhood spokespeople, university representatives, and other interested parties have agreed to the nonconforming use, I will support this use before the planning board and city council. I hope that the spirit of cooperation we have started here will grow and that we can solve other problems in the city in this same manner.

Discussion Questions

1. How could the city manager have avoided public disagreement with the planning director?
2. At this point, should the city manager
   a. Ignore the planning director's public disagreement and chalk up his opposition to the director's sense of professionalism?
   b. Confront and discipline the planning director over his public disagreement?
   c. Fire the planning director?
   d. Reexamine his relationship with his department heads?
3. Assume you are the planning director. What would you have said to this assembled group? Would you have supported the nonconforming use or opposed it?

4. Do you think the planning director's sense of professionalism should outweigh the city manager's attempts to foster a cooperative solution to this problem?
5. Do you think the city manager's attempts to create a cooperative environment between university and neighborhood interests are more important than the technical requirements of the zoning code?
6. What interests do the four groups of stakeholders—university, downtown business owners, neighborhood activists, and the city—share? And what interests do you think they might disagree on?
7. In general, what are other scenarios in which a technical expert is likely to differ with the city manager?
8. What if the difference of opinion had occurred between the city manager and a council member instead of between the manager and a subordinate? What would the consequences be?

Suggested Simulation Roles

Minimum Roles Needed for Simulation

Assistant to the university chancellor
Head of neighborhood association
Several neighborhood residents
City manager
Director of city planning department

Other Possible Roles

University chancellor
Several downtown business owners
Police chief
University students

6

Theft in an Elective Office

Jack Manahan

Background

Alec Stokesville had been manager of Encouragement, a Midwestern government of 225,000 people, for nearly a year. Encouragement's organization was complex, with eleven governing body members and twenty-four departments, including several elected department heads and a few more-or-less independent agencies with their own governing boards. Sometimes he found himself worrying more about the process to get things done than what actually should be done. Nevertheless, he was enjoying the job enormously and by all accounts was doing an excellent job. With Thanksgiving only a week away, he was looking forward to spending the holiday with his family.

He was jolted from his reverie by the ringing phone. "It's Frances Powell," his executive assistant said. Problems in the organization were hard to keep secret, and he was pretty sure why Powell, who was the treasurer, was calling. Some irregularities had been discovered in one of the treasurer's accounts, and suspicion lay on a clerk who had quit a few months ago.

Powell was one of the elected department heads who did not report to Stokesville. Her office handled all investments and revenue collection. It also handled court records and money, which was substantial: about $4 million in court fees, fines, and bond money passed through the office each year. The finance department, which did report to him, was responsible for accounting, financial reporting, accounts payable, and payroll.

Powell had been a governing body member until about seven years ago, when she was elected treasurer. Her term of office was up the next fall. Although she had not announced her plans, most observers expected her to run for another term as treasurer.

"Hello, Frances," Alec said. "I understand we may have some problems down there."

"News travels fast," she replied. "I need to see you as soon as possible. Can I come up?"

When Powell arrived in his office, she told him that the loss had been discovered when a clerk in the office had tried to enter a disbursement, ordered by one of the judges, to close out a case file. According to the computer record, the bond money had already been returned to the defendant. Powell's staff alerted her, and she had already called the state's attorney and police. She told Stokesville they were still trying to sort out what happened, but it appeared to be more than simply a computer error. A summit meeting was quickly convened with Stokesville, Powell, the chief of detectives, the state's attorney, the outside auditors, and the data processing staff person who handled the judicial system computer program.

The group discussed ways to investigate the extent of the loss. Powell told the group that she had already done a quick review of some of the closed court files, and her signature appeared to have been forged on disbursement authorizations in several files. Although the evidence seemed to point to the former employee, they wondered whether the former employee's guilt could actually be proven. For now, the group could do nothing other than let the detectives do their job.

The next day, those with knowledge of theft were relieved to learn that when detectives questioned the former clerk, she admitted to the crime and was taken into custody. Although she wasn't sure exactly how much she had taken over her 18 months in the treasurer's office, she thought it was around $10,000.

Upon the arrest of the ex-employee, Stokesville suggested to Powell that she call a news conference to disclose the loss and the arrest. The theme of Powell's announcement to the media was that strong internal controls in her department had uncovered the theft, and the story quickly faded from the news.

The Case

In January there is another loss in the treasurer's office—this time about $1,500 in cash. With several clerks using the same cash drawer, investigators cannot determine the culprit or the method, and so there are no arrests.

Meanwhile, working with the treasurer's staff, detectives, and the outside auditors, staff from data processing are able to develop an automated query of all inactive court files to analyze the discrepancies. The analysis shows that the loss discovered last fall was not $10,000 but actually closer to $60,000. In the course of the investigation, the detectives also discover that the ex-employee had declared bankruptcy, and she had been investigated but not charged with theft in another state before being hired by Powell.

The ex-employee agrees to plead guilty. She is ordered to pay restitution but given a suspended sentence. She pays $15,000 immediately and agrees to pay the rest in installments. Encouragement's insurance carrier considers each instance of theft contributing to the $60,000 total to be a separate claim, and no single claim exceeds Encouragement's crime-bond retention amount. Thus the remainder of the stolen money—$45,000—is a potential hit on the treasury, one case at a time, pending full restitution.

As predicted, Frances Powell decides to run for reelection. A highly popular politician, she has no challengers from her party in the April primary. However, three challengers from the other party announce plans to run. One is Harry Lewis, a veteran member of the governing body. Lewis wins his party's primary and therefore will face Powell in the November general election.

Following the April primary, Powell agrees to Stokesville's recommendation for an internal organizational review of the financial management function. Stokesville offers staff from his office and the personnel department to form the review team. He also suggests adding the outside auditors to the team to review cash-handling and internal controls in the office. Powell agrees, and Stokesville briefs governing body members on the plan.

In the review team's report, several internal control issues surface relating to segregation of financial duties. The report recommends that the office be reorganized, with all bookkeepers and cashiers now reporting to a chief cashier rather than division heads. In addition, the report recommends more training for clerks and bookkeepers. Despite the government's tight finances, Stokesville adds two positions for the treasurer in his recommended budget: the chief cashier and a bookkeeper to further segregate financial duties among the staff.

Over the summer, a series of small but nevertheless embarrassing incidents keeps the treasurer's office in the news. A current employee is accused by a customer of marking a fine "paid" and pocketing the money. Because the office is shorthanded, Powell does not suspend the clerk during the investigation.

In another episode, an attorney is caught attempting to remove documents, presumably damaging to his client's case, from a case file—a file to which he should not have had unsupervised access. Then a piece of evidence in a criminal case disappears from the evidence locker. Despite Powell's assertions the previous November following discovery of the first theft, it is becoming evident that strong internal controls are lacking and the office management remains slack.

Stokesville infers from his sources in the building that there is common knowledge of how to steal money. With almost constant turnover in some positions, the office is continually short staffed and in the control of a few of the old-timers, only some of them faithful, capable workers. Several of the more recent hires appear to be poor performers, yet Powell seems unwilling to hurt their feelings by counseling them. Because Powell is an elected official, her treasurer's office handles its own personnel matters. To date, the governing body has shown little interest in persuading her to adopt the personnel and administrative policies that apply to appointed department managers.

The partner in charge of the annual audit expresses his concern to Stokesville that, despite continued reminders and training, bookkeepers in the treasurer's office are months behind in reconciling the office's bank statements. As a result, auditing the treasurer's records each year has become increasingly difficult. The audit partner further informs Stokesville that under the new internal control standards for government audits, he will have no choice in the next audit but to report on significant internal control deficiencies.

The Decision Problem

After Labor Day, the fall election campaign heats up. Without attacking Powell's integrity, Harry Lewis nevertheless mounts a strong campaign for treasurer, predicated on the need for change in the office. Whether in spite of or because of the forthcoming election, some members of the governing body and other officials, including the state's attorney and the chief judge, are becoming openly concerned about the operation of the treasurer's office and the protection of court records and evidence.

Stokesville considers his alternatives, and none of them are very good. He has already provided Powell with additional staff to improve the office's operations. However, she has yet to take any action to hire for the new positions. Few of the recommended procedural changes have been made and he has no ability to force Powell to make changes.

He could "throw her overboard" and take the position that the problems are Powell's alone to solve. However, if he doesn't try to help Powell, the good working relationships he's worked to develop with the other elected department heads could be damaged.

He considers the time and effort it would take to change the treasurer's position to an appointed one that reports to the manager: several months of behind-the-scenes work to get the governing body members even comfortable with the idea. Formal approval would have to come next. He would have to get the question onto an election ballot and organize a successful referendum. Then, even if the vote were successful, the change would not take place until the end of the treasurer's next term of office. All in all, it could take at least five years.

Moreover, any actions he might take now could affect the outcome of the election. Regardless of his personal leanings, Stokesville's professional code of ethics precludes his involvement or interference in electoral politics.

However, the public's confidence in the government and the judicial system, the integrity of its assets and records, and the stewardship of public funds are at stake. If he fails to take action, Stokesville believes that the governing body and his administration will be vulnerable to criticism. In addition, anything less than a clean, unqualified audit opinion could affect Encouragement's bond rating and thus its ability to access capital markets at favorable interest rates—essential for financing upcoming capital projects.

Two weeks before the election, Treasurer Powell finally fires her chief deputy and announces her intent to recruit a chief cashier position to oversee day-to-day cash management and bookkeeping.

In the November election, veteran political observers in the community are stunned that despite the bad publicity about the losses and mismanagement in her office, Powell wins another term by a narrow margin. A vote cast by Harry Lewis for an unpopular issue at a governing body meeting just before the election was apparently the deciding factor. However, by the end of the following March, Powell still has not hired a chief cashier, and few concrete improvements have been accomplished.

Discussion Questions

1. The treasurer's office is headed by an elected official, Frances Powell, who does not report through the chain of command to the governing body or the manager. Are any of the events that have transpired truly Manager Alec Stokesville's problem?
2. Do you think that Stokesville was wise to suggest that Powell hold a news conference to announce discovery of the first theft? Why or why not?
3. Is Stokesville truly powerless to effect any change in the treasurer's office? Are there any alternatives, either short term or long term, that he has overlooked to improve the management and operation of the office? Are his options after the election different from his options just before it?
4. Solutions in complex organizations often involve other parties. Presuming that Stokesville should become involved in reorganizing the treasurer's office, who else should be involved, and what are the trade-offs between a concern for urgency and a concern for process?

Suggested Simulation Roles

Alec Stokesville, manager
Frances Powell, treasurer
Governing body members
Chief detective
Outside audit partner
Harry Lewis, candidate for treasurer
Chief judge

Part III

Enhancing the Governing Body's Effectiveness

Introduction to Part III

Enhancing the Governing Body's Effectiveness

A half century ago, the typical local government manager had the luxury of a governing body that was part time and willing to take the advice of the manager on operational matters. Today, many governing bodies are overly political: often members are elected because of a single issue they either advocated for or promised to work against. Moreover, the task of operating a government is far more complex today for many reasons: more functions to perform, intricate networks involving other governments and private organizations, competition for human and fiscal resources, and diversity in the workforce, to name a few.

In this more complex political environment, much is expected of the local government manager: (1) to bring well-conceived policy recommendations to the council or board, (2) to help members work through their differences to arrive at effective public policy, and (3) to minimize conflicts stemming from the fact that the governing body is elected, whereas staff members are professionals hired for their technical knowledge and skills.

Techniques of citizen involvement—both representational ones such as citizen surveys and more direct ones such as public hearings—must complement methods for helping governing body members understand the issues. The manager must be careful not to overwhelm the governing body with technical details but at the same time must give elected officials sufficient relevant information for making wise decisions. The manager must also be prepared to be a negotiator, both between staff and council and between council and interested citizen and business groups.

Cases 7, 8, and 9 explore how a manager can help the community's governing body to develop sound public policy and procedures. Case 7, "Political Ambitions versus the Public Good," involves a confrontation between older, less affluent residents and wealthier, younger newcomers to a quaint community. Two major problems are the increase in property values—and in property taxes—brought about by growth and the resulting decrease in affordable housing. The search for a solution to the problem of affordable housing is complicated by the presence of a highly ambitious elected official who uses the affordable housing issue and its racial implications to launch his campaign for mayor. Worst of all, the resulting controversy has become fodder for the national media.

Case 8, "Riding the Development Dragon," addresses another development issue from the standpoint of the council's role as protector of the community's financial health. An annexation proposed by a forcign developer offers the community a chance to double in size. However, as is often the case with large-scale projects, the developer wants a number of financial concessions from the community. For its part, the community is concerned about whether the project will actually be completed. The community-wide excitement around anticipated growth is tempered by financial constraints and the increasing demands of the developer.

The third case in the section, Case 9, "The Chief versus the Council Member," illustrates the strains on the relationship between a department head and the council when change is afoot. A new, highly professional police chief replaces a popular good old boy in a suburban city. The new chief wants to ensure that his department exemplifies professional behavior in every sense: ethics, procedures, personnel actions. When the chief tries to institute new rules for officer behavior, the manager faces several obstacles: rebellion from rank-and-file officers, involvement by the American Civil Liberties Union, and threats from a council member.

Cases in Part III emphasize a number of management practices: policy facilitation, citizen service, democratic advocacy and citizen participation, diversity, human resource management, financial analysis, and integrity. Consequently, analyzing the cases gives the reader an opportunity to develop skills needed to help the governing body be more effective.

7

Political Ambitions versus the Public Good

Jerry Kloby

Background

Green Mountain is a municipality of 40,000 citizens with a council-manager form of government. The town is home to families who have lived there for generations as well as newcomers attracted by the quaint older homes, tree-lined streets, and an exceptional magnet school system. The demand for housing significantly increased upon completion of a new train line providing direct access to a major nearby city. Thus the reputation of the town and the convenient commute to the city combined to create a surge in housing costs that resulted in a crisis for many township residents. Compounding the problem are rising property taxes (the main source of funding for the school system), which add to the cost of housing for both homeowners and renters.

Green Mountain is diverse in many respects. Nearly one-third of the town's residents are African American, though the proportion of Hispanics and Asians is lower than both the national and regional averages. The median household income of Green Mountain is well above the national average, and to some extent the high median obscures the economic diversity of the town. Based on the last U.S. census, 13 percent of Green Mountain's households had incomes above $200,000. However, 15 percent fell below $25,000, and nearly 25 percent were below $35,000. Approximately 56 percent of all housing units are owner-occupied and 44 percent are renter-occupied.

In addition, the town is a mix of long-time residents and big-city newcomers. The latter, who are better able to afford the higher housing costs, are often unaware of the local struggles to maintain the town's character. Part of that character is Green Mountain's diverse housing stock, which many view as crucial to maintaining the economic, racial, age, and other diversities that enrich the town.

Two months before the events of this case, two Green Mountain residents who were affiliated with a national nonprofit devoted to housing and community development published an op-ed piece in the town newspaper calling for an "equitable development commission." The article by Robert Knight and Al Shamsky cited anecdotal evidence about rising housing costs and suggested five policy options that the town could pursue.

At that time, the face of the problem for many residents was the demolition of the local bowling alley to make room for 70 upscale one- and two-bedroom apartments with monthly rents ranging from $1,800 to $2,600. On a square-foot basis, the new apartments were the most expensive in the entire town. One of the options

Knight and Shamsky proposed was to create a local affordable housing trust fund that would be financed by a fee on new development.

The developer failed to include any units in the new complex that would be affordable to individuals of low or moderate incomes. This omission was seen as a portent of things to come: small housing units, high prices, increased congestion, more wealthy professionals, fewer family-friendly homes and neighborhoods, and lack of affordable housing for young people who had grown up in Green Mountain and wished to remain there. For town officials, however, these types of housing units represented greater property tax revenues without the correspondingly large expenses for services such as garbage pickup and expanded school enrollments.

Although most residents might tacitly have tolerated the stylish brick apartments shoehorned into the site of the old bowling alley, a precipitating event sparked town-wide consciousness of Green Mountain's housing crisis. That event was the attempted eviction of tenants in a six-unit building just a short walk from the new Bay Ridge train station. The eviction attempt was brought to the attention of the local chapter of the National Association for the Advancement of Colored People who, in dramatic style, demanded that the town's leaders do something about the simmering housing affordability crisis.

This event served as a wake-up call for the mayor and town council. Town Manager Michael Bradford was struck both by the audacity of the landlord in the case and the groundswell of community support that rallied around the tenants. The eviction notices had followed on the heels of the landlord's attempt to get the tenants to sign yearlong leases that would have raised their rents by several hundred dollars a month. The tenants, of course, refused.

Under pressure from the NAACP, the mayor investigated the landlord's claim that the wholesale eviction was required by the utility company to upgrade an inadequate heating system. After speaking to utility company authorities the mayor concluded that the landlord's claim was unfounded, and he directed the township attorney to order the landlord to cease and desist its eviction attempts, on the grounds that they were based on "deceptive business practices" and did not comply with the state's eviction laws.

The Case

As the township manager, Bradford knows the concerns of long-term residents, who for years have seen their property taxes rise at a disturbing rate and whose grown children often were unable to buy or rent in the township due to rising prices. He is also hearing from tenants who have little protection against rising rents and evictions—the result of gentrification triggered by the new train line. Many residents have attended town meetings just to voice their frustrations and fears.

The seven-member council is divided on what to do, although all council members recognize that the housing issue is a hot-button item. Some members think the town has done more than a reasonable person would expect to promote affordable housing. By the town's own count, approximately 700 housing units (out of 15,000) are available to people of low income (defined as less than 50 percent of the area median). On the one hand, council members realize that an influx of higher-income residents will do more to enhance property tax revenues and relieve some of the pressure to cut municipal expenditures. On the other hand, many of those caught in the housing squeeze are constituents to whom council representatives feel an obligation. In short, for any council member, getting caught on the wrong side of the issue would have political consequences. Moreover, the housing controversy is now the subject of regular articles in the town's weekly newspaper and is occasionally making headlines in one of the state's largest dailies. Eventually, it even draws the attention of a major national newspaper.

As one of its first steps in dealing with the crisis, the council adopts the innovative and relatively uncontroversial affordable housing trust fund initiative proposed by Green Mountain residents Knight and Shamsky. In spite of this action, the council knows the trust fund option is a limited one. It will not soon generate any money, and ahead lies the complex task of deciding on the types of projects that the fund should finance.

Community leaders continue to press for more action even as the town council seeks ways to respond. Michael Bradford, however, has learned something very important from the trust fund proposal. In his position as town manager he frequently hears citizen complaints about inadequate snow removal or garbage pickup, shortcomings in the town's recycling plans, issues of fairness in hiring and promotion for township jobs, and the like. Frequently, the complaints come from a relatively small but vocal contingent. The contentious exchanges create a temptation for Bradford to minimize his public interaction. But in the case of the affordable housing trust fund, here was a very good idea that originated with local residents with some expertise in the issue.

Now Bradford sees an opportunity to create a different kind of dialogue with the town's residents—a productive discussion that departs from his more typical dealings with the squeaky wheels who show up at council meetings and persistently call his office. Now he wonders if a more systematic, broad-based attempt to increase public input might engage residents who have positive contributions to make and result in a more objective assessment of the housing situation. He is highly supportive, although somewhat apprehensive, as over the next few months the council

- Adopts a carefully worded resolution stating that the issue of housing affordability is a shared problem. The resolution acknowledges the contribution that diversity makes in enriching the lives of residents; fostering civic participation; and making possible a vibrant business, artistic, and educational environment. The council resolves to take steps to promote housing affordability as a way of maintaining Green Mountain's diversity.
- Creates an affordable housing task force composed of two council members; the town manager; the town planner; and representatives of numerous stakeholders including community activists, housing experts, civil rights leaders, nonprofit leaders, and landlords.
- Sponsors a well-publicized speak-out to engage citizens in an open dialogue about the problems and possible solutions.
- Holds a daylong housing conference with eight workshops—all open to the public—on specialized topics such as options for financing affordable housing, tenant rights, and land-use strategies. Each workshop features one or two invited participants from around the state with some expertise in the topic. Showing foresight, the new affordable housing task force designs the workshops so they can morph into working groups that will ultimately make policy recommendations.
- Commits to developing a strategic master housing plan and hires a consulting firm with national experience to document the extent of the housing affordability problem in Green Mountain. The firm also will make detailed recommendations and suggestions.

Clearly these actions show that the mayor and council have taken significant steps to engage residents in a dialogue that should, ideally, result in a collaborative effort to find possible remedies.

However, Manager Bradford is privately concerned about the politics of the process. Council member Ted Lang has taken a leadership role, working with him to organize the public events. Some suspect that Councilman Lang is ambitious for higher office: at social events he has been spotted in long conversations with members of the business community and several developers. Meanwhile, some community leaders are seeing a backlash developing against the affordable housing movement. Despite his hopes that Councilman Lang can balance the divergent interest groups, Bradford fears that Lang's obvious political aspirations may compromise his ability both to listen to citizens and to present to the mayor and council policy alternatives that can make a positive impact.

Bradford realizes that the consulting firm is one of the keys to building consensus and defusing the resistance coming his way from landlords and realtors. He is relieved to find the firm very thorough and professional. After several months of meetings with various parties, including sessions with the postconference working groups, as well as collecting a large amount of quantitative data, the consulting firm does an excellent job of documenting the extent of the problem and the implications of housing trends for the principle of diversity. Overall, the findings validate the perceptions that housing affordability has eroded, and the final report is able to quantify the impact in a way that community leaders could not. The consulting firm also works with the affordable housing task force to elucidate the main principles motivating the task force.

Guiding Principles Defined by the Green Mountain Affordable Housing Task Force:

- Maintain and enhance community character and quality of life.
- Maximize housing choices to maintain community diversity.
- Distribute affordable housing throughout the township.
- Focus new development in and around transit hubs and corridors.
- Meet workforce housing needs.
- Preserve existing affordable units.
- Strive for "affordability in perpetuity."

Findings and Recommendations

The yearlong efforts of Green Mountain's affordable housing task force and the hired consultant produce a thoroughly documented, seventy-two-page "Affordable Housing Strategy" with specific policy recommendations.

First, the consultant's research confirms that Green Mountain's problem of housing affordability is serious. Approximately 3,750 households out of 15,000 were living in unaffordable or inadequate housing at the time of the last census, and since then housing costs have risen sharply. Green Mountain is losing its diversity. The firm finds significant out-migration of seniors, with a loss of 1,400 seniors over the past ten years. There is also a decline in the number of young adults living in the town, while recent school-lunch participation rates show an out-migration of lower-income families with children. Neighborhoods that traditionally provided affordable housing are being gentrified, affordable family housing throughout the town is endangered, and senior housing options also are limited.

In terms of race and ethnicity, however, the consultants find slightly more diversity in Green Mountain than was seen ten years earlier. The proportion of African Americans rose from 31 percent to 33 percent; the percentage of Asians rose from 2 percent to 3 percent; and the Hispanic population rose from 3 percent to 5 percent.

The biggest changes have to do with economic diversity. Overall, the portion of the population in the upper-income brackets ($100,000 to 500,000, and $500,000+) is growing, and the percent of residents below the poverty line has dropped. (The report acknowledges that the official poverty rate has one serious shortcoming: it does not account for regional variations in cost of living). By local standards nearly 40 percent of Green Mountain's households are considered low or moderate income. ("Low-income" is defined in terms of households with incomes of less than 50 percent of the township's median income. Moderate-income households are those falling between 50 percent and 80 percent of the median.)

The consulting firm documents the financial hardship that the housing crisis has created for many residents. At the time of the last census, approximately 30 percent of homeowners and 33 percent of renters overpaid for housing—that is, they were paying more than 30 percent of their income for housing. Among low-income renters (those with household income of less than $35,000), nearly 75 percent were overpaying for housing, with 60 percent paying more than 35 percent of their income. For moderate-income households (between $35,000 and $50,000), 64 percent of homeowners were overpaying.

The incidence of overpayment has increased since the last Census.

Overall, the consulting firm concludes that

> ...there are extremely few market-rate units in Green Mountain that remain affordable to lower income households and that moderate income households would be most impacted by the price increases of the past three years...It is not unrealistic to expect that the incidence of overpayment for this group is now in the range of 50 percent. In Green Mountain, a significant majority of low and moderate households are living in unaffordable housing situations, with nearly all low income households (25 percent of the township's households) lacking affordable housing.

The consulting firm makes its recommendations, each one including a detailed series of practical steps that should be taken.

Consultant's Recommendations:

1. Establish a full-time housing specialist position to implement the policy recommendations.
2. Create a housing commission.
3. Adopt an inclusionary zoning provision for new construction.
4. Create partnerships for development with nonprofit housing agencies and private sector developers.
5. Promote the rehabilitation of deteriorating housing to improve quality and preserve affordability.
6. Develop a clear procedure for dispute resolution under a strengthened and reconstituted rent arbitration board.
7. Establish a community land trust, using nonprofit ownership as a vehicle for ensuring long-term affordability of housing.
8. Employ community outreach and education to engender involvement and support for the housing strategy.

The Decision Problem

Eighteen months after the affordable housing strategy report comes out, Manager Bradford is disturbed by three things:

1. Important recommendations are removed from the final strategy as a result of pressure from private interests and Councilman Ted Lang.

2. Lang uses the process to launch a successful campaign for mayor.
3. In his first year in office, Mayor Lang has failed to follow through on a number of the strategy's key recommendations.

The first of the three happened when the consulting firm, under pressure from landlords on the affordable housing task force, agreed to remove discussion of rent regulation from its final report. In a separate memo, the consultant explained his decision.

> [G]iven time constraints and the contention and emotion surrounding rent control, the decision was taken to remove rent regulation from the Green Mountain affordable housing strategy policy options.... Including rent regulation in the strategic plan would divert attention from other policy issues and decisions, including ones that I believe are most important for long-term affordability.

The decision to strip rent regulation from the strategy meant that it would be much more difficult, if not impossible, for the town to implement comprehensive regulations to protect Green Mountain's large number of renters. The loss of that language also undermined the work of the rent regulation working group, which was the hardest-working group to emerge from the housing conference. The rent regulation working group evaluated numerous research reports on different types of rent controls enacted around the nation. Rather than simply giving a thumbs-up or thumbs-down to rent control, it carefully assessed specific provisions within laws, ultimately developing an authoritative outline of best practices for rent regulation. It also had to bear the brunt of landlord opposition to the movement to keep Green Mountain affordable.

The consulting firm's memo on rent regulation ultimately endorsed every aspect of the rent regulation plan created by the working group. The consultants stated that

> a moderate rent regulation ordinance—as proposed by the rent regulation working group—can be an effective tool for Green Mountain in helping slow the displacement of lower income households from the township, and to guard against the more significant displacement that can result during periods of rapid rent increases. It can achieve this at little monetary cost to the township, and with little to no effect on housing quality, new construction, or property taxes.

However, instead of recommending a rent regulation ordinance in the affordable housing strategy, the consultant recommended that Green Mountain establish a rent arbitration board to replace the Landlord-Tenant Advisory Committee (LTAC) that had been in existence for over twenty years. Those few tenants who knew about it largely regarded the LTAC as biased and almost completely ineffective at protecting them.

The rent arbitration board, as proposed, could make binding decisions on disputes between tenants and landlords. It would be responsible for collecting accurate information about rents in the town, broken down by unit type and location—data sorely lacking in the public discussion about soaring housing costs. But the rent arbitration board never got off the ground. Other key recommendations were ignored as well.

Though Mayor Lang continued to espouse the principles of the affordable housing strategy, under his leadership the town council took only a few of the steps recommended by the consultant. A housing commission was established but the position of housing specialist was never created. An inclusionary zoning ordinance passed, but it was weaker than the minimum recommended. The mayor and council did nothing to strengthen and reconstitute a rent arbitration board, nor did they take steps to create a community land trust. The consultant's separate memo endorsing moderate rent regulation was buried for good.

Now, Manager Bradford faces two problematic decisions: what to do about the housing issue and how to work with Mayor Lang.

Discussion Questions

1. What were the risks, benefits, and drawbacks of Manager Bradford's engaging so many people in the policy making process?
2. Could the manager have influenced Lang's actions as chair of the task force?
3. Could the manager have minimized the effect of private interests that were intent on subverting the work of the task force?
4. Given that the process was highly inclusive, does that fact now help or hurt Bradford's chances for promoting implementation of the consultant's recommendations?
5. What obligation does the manager have to implement the affordable housing strategy?
6. Should the manager pursue the rent regulation recommendations that were omitted from the overall strategy?
7. Is there anything Manager Bradford can do now to encourage the council to implement the recommendations of the affordable housing strategy?
8. Should the manager be proactive regarding the policy recommendations that have not been pursued?
9. What steps could the town manager take to build some agreement and support to protect tenants? What tools does he have at his disposal?
10. Mayor Lang will be in office for at least two more years. Should this fact play into Manager Bradford's decision making?

Suggested Simulation Roles

Create a simulation in which the town manager presents the case for implementing the unfulfilled recommendations of Green Mountain's affordable housing strategy to the housing commission. On the housing commission be sure to include the following roles:

- a chair who tries to be balanced and to uphold the principles of the commission and the affordable housing strategy
- a strong advocate for the strategy
- a strong advocate for tenants
- a representative of a nonprofit housing or community development organization
- a representative of landlord or realtor interests
- a civil rights advocate.

Other roles can be added to expand the simulation, such as

- the town's chief financial officer
- other public officials.

Have the observers of this presentation and subsequent discussion evaluate the case made by the manager. They should offer suggestions for building consensus. Discuss what issues or matters can be compromised and what principles should be inviolate.

Riding the Development Dragon

Gary L. Sears

This case is based on the challenges facing a newly hired public administrator in a primarily rural mountain community of 1,500 people called Rosedale. Rosedale has been incorporated for 13 years and is considered a relatively new town in the region. Rosedale is addressing a proposal for development and annexation of 3,000 acres of land, which will double the land area of the community and will require an extensive legal agreement and extensive staff review and follow-up in the implementation of the annexation and development agreement.

Kelly McGee, with 10 years of public management experience and a master of public administration degree, has been hired to be the first town manager. The town attorney was the one to suggest hiring a town manager because he thought that implementing an annexation agreement would be impossible without a professional manager to negotiate details of the ensuing development and manage the town day to day. Because McGee grew up in a nearby town, he is familiar with the characteristics and development requirements of mountain communities.

Background

Rosedale is situated in a historic and scenic part of the state. The community is comprised of longtime residents, small-business owners providing various services to the resorts in the area, and some construction and mining families working for the highway department and the region's hard-rock mining companies. Further, the town supports the many environmental issues of the region by serving as the area headquarters of the Rosewood Forest Services as well as the county headquarters of the federal Bureau of Land Management.

The recent growth in Rosedale's population is partly attributable to the influx of young families employed in the recreational, government, and real estate industries. However, other residents commute over 120 miles a day to a major metropolitan community. These commuters tend to oppose any development that would reduce their perceived quality of life in Rosedale.

The viewpoints of this very diverse population are reflected on the town board. At the time of the town manager's hiring, board members included a construction worker, a mining engineer, a corporate engineer (who had lived in the town for 10 years and commuted to a large engineering office in the metropolitan city every day), the waste management supervisor (also the mayor), the former town clerk, an auto body repairman, and a high school teacher. Because of its diversity, the town board is considered credible by the citizens of Rosedale even though it has not been involved in either an annexation or development of a sizable property.

Town Manager McGee, on the other hand, anticipates difficulty meeting the conflicting interests of the town population and the town board. His best line of defense is probably to work quickly with the members of the town board to establish a consensus in the community about the development. Clearly the project will pose its share of contentious land use, environmental, and construction management issues.

McGee is realistic about his strengths and weaknesses. Before coming to Rosedale he worked in several communities as an assistant manager; however, he has only limited experience in working with key planning or construction issues associated with this type of development. His skill set favors general public administration, and he knows he will need to tap into those skills to assemble a successful team. He and that team must work through the many technical aspects involved in reviewing and approving the proposed development.

When he was hired by the town, the town had only twelve full-time staff members, including a finance manager and planning director. The part-time public works director also worked for a local engineering firm. The town had a contract with the town attorney, who reported directly to the town board. In addition, several private consultants had capably supported the town's utilities, finance, construction management, and legal needs. Thus far, the town board has been satisfied with these consultants' help in facing the challenges of this complex development proposal.

The development agreement incorporates several of the town's critical issues: (1) preservation of the water quality on the site and in the adjacent river; (2) protection of the watershed and riparian areas on the site; (3) water pressure and the additional fill required to prevent the freezing of water and wastewater lines; (4) the interface of utilities and roadways with the adjacent subdivisions; (5) adequate snow removal and adequate street width to accommodate snowplowing in the winter and bicycle lanes in the summer; and (6) the brief construction season.

The Developers

The Far East Development Company Inc. has recently purchased the Sky Hawk Ridge property—3,000 acres adjacent to Rosedale. An investment company in Hong Kong is funding the purchase and planned development. In early discussions with the town, principals of the development company claim they are well funded and eager to construct the required improvements for the development. Several of them are from the Hong Kong area, and during these early meetings they often speak in Cantonese among themselves. Town manager McGee finds it difficult to understand the nuances of their concerns, and he further suspects that the principals are not familiar with the unique aspects of development in mountainous terrain.

As McGee reviews the background of the development company, he learns that it has never worked in the United States. Most of its development experience has been in Southeast Asia. This discovery solidifies his view that the company will have trouble understanding the nature of the costs and construction issues that come with development at 8,000 feet above sea level. Because the Rosedale area lacks a strong supply of qualified contractors, McGee and his staff predict that that many of the developer's cost projections are too low to meet the development expectations of the community.

Very early in the development process, the Far East Development Company's principals inform the town that that they must rely on its staff and consultants to help them develop the property. As an example, to reduce costs and to expedite the development, the town board and the developer agree that the town attorney will write the development agreements and the developer will reimburse the town attorney for his work. However, some citizens express concern that the developer is benefiting more than the town in this arrangement and that the town's interests are not being fully represented by the town attorney. Conversely, the developer expresses dissatisfaction with the cost of the legal services and the "lack of representation" by the town's attorney in favor of the developer on critical issues. However, in the interest of "expediting the process," the developer continues using and paying for the services of the town attorney, as approved in the original agreement.

In addition, from early on, the principals frequently have asked the manager and town board members what they need to pay the town up front to avoid excessive development regulations. They imply that this practice is common in Southeast Asia.

As a way of introducing themselves to the town, the Far East Development Company representatives hosted a "getting to know you meal" at one of the best restaurants in the area for the entire town board, planning commission, staff, and their respective spouses. Recalling this event has reinforced the town manager's view that challenging ethical issues lie ahead. McGee expects that the Far East Development Company will seek many concessions from the town during the review and development processes.

Despite these several concerns, he and the town board are excited about the prospect of bringing a large, comprehensive development to the community—more prestigious, indeed, than the smaller subdivisions of the past.

The Case

The area to be developed borders the Rosewood National Forest on two sides. It shares another border with mountain property that could eventually be annexed to Rosedale. At this point Sky Hawk Ridge has no homes—only a few dirt roads criss-crossing it. However, it offers breathtaking views of the mountains and a river that divides the ridge, not to mention proximity to several resort areas. The town board and most of the community hope that if the property can be successfully developed—especially with its projected new golf course, scenic homesites, and commercial areas—it will transform the Rosedale community into more of a resort community, like other cities in the region.

However, the town manager also knows that some in the community plan to fight the development because it could spell—at least short term—reductions in town service levels, more costs to local residents, and reductions in the quality of life for existing residents. McGee agrees to himself that the community could be overwhelmed by the issues associated with this development. He will have to work closely with all elements—community, staff, and consultants—to make sure that the agreements and construction ultimately work to preserve Rosedale's character and protect and improve the community at large.

Here is a summary of how the community and board view the development following numerous public meetings about Sky Hawk Ridge.

The pro-development group sees the following benefits:

1. The development will bring prosperity to the area.
2. The development will complement the rural nature of the town because it will be a resort development. Over time it will fulfill its destiny to become a mountain recreation and vacation center in the region.
3. The development will support the small businesses of the area.
4. The development will improve the reputation of the community by elevating it to a resort community, as opposed to what some thought was "just a town of trailer parks and service workers."

The anti-development group has these concerns:

1. The developer may not have the resources to finish the project because of its lack of experience in developing a mountainous area.

2. The new development will affect the water supply and mountain vistas and could be detrimental to the fragile mountain environment.
3. The character of the town will change to "just another resort town."
4. The new development will not fit into the historic character of this western, independent community.
5. The quality of town services will suffer, and taxes will increase to subsidize this proposed new development.

After considering the arguments of both sides, the town board agrees to a master development agreement with the developer. It consists of three phases of development based on the terrain. Each phase will have to be approved by the town board before the project could continue. The agreement also permits the use of a "metropolitan district" funding method, using taxes and fees from the development to pay for the site's infrastructure. Last, the agreement requires the developer to pay tap fees (plant investment fees) to the town up front for each phase of the project, thus defraying the town's share of the cost of necessary capital improvements.

Soon after agreeing to the master development agreement but before the start of construction, the developer informs the town that the up-front costs are much greater than expected. The company asks to defer the initial tap fees (several hundreds of thousands of dollars) until the second phase of the project. Reluctantly and over the protests of the town manager and several staff members, the board votes 4 to 3 to delay this required payment.

As the project progresses, the developer continues to seek concessions. Town meetings become more heated and contentious; however, there is also a sense of more pressure being applied to keep the development moving. Several board members have stated publicly that the staff "is not being flexible enough and is not accommodating the interests of the developer." One of these board members is emphatic that "the staff should not be an obstacle but should give the Far East Development Company anything they need to keep the project moving." Another board member threatens, "If this project does not proceed according to the interests of the developer, heads will roll and many staff members and consultants will need to be replaced."

At every turn, the developer challenges the staff and consultants, voicing dismay at the projected costs of bringing the development to completion. Its representatives reiterate that their firm cannot afford the excessive costs being proposed by the staff. They repeatedly contend that the town should use its own funds as well as lower some of its standards "to support this important annexation and development to Rosedale."

The development's impact on the rural, recreational, and scenic aspects of the current town remains a hot button, with one citizens' faction demanding more planning and review on each phase. Fears persist that the impact of increasing population, cars, construction, costs for expanded utilities, and the like on the community will ruin its quality of life and blemish its history.

A mining widow known only as Winnie, living in a small house next to the town hall, was once spotted throwing stones at the town's first paving machine as the contractor was applying asphalt to her street. Other longtime residents, angry about the prospect of this new development, show up at town meetings to demand an end to the project. It will, they say, ruin their fishing areas, hiking trails, and mountain vistas—not to mention the rural character of the town.

In response, several town board members agree that more oversight is needed for the design and construction of the amenities project, and they voice support for slowing down the review process. Furthermore, these board members threatened to vote down the second phase of the development unless the project meets improved environmental and construction standards.

The Decision Problem

As they prepare to consider approval of the second phase, the town administrator and board receive a letter from the Far East Development Company. It states that the developer "cannot continue the development unless the town agrees to delay the payment of tap fees until the final phase of development, especially considering that the fees were not frozen by the town in the master plan agreement."

To address the developer's refusal to pay the tap fees (amounting to several hundreds of thousands of dollars), the board schedules a special meeting. In addition, it asks Town Manager McGee for his recommendation on the proposed approval of the second phase of development (in effect, his recommendation on whether to continue the project).

In preparation for the upcoming special meeting, the town manager meets with staff, the mayor, and key community groups; reviews the critical issues associated with the continuation or termination of the project; and prepares his recommendation. Here is a summary of the issues Rosedale faces in deciding whether to approve phase two of the master development agreement.

1. *Cost and quality.* The costs for inspection, redesign, and approval of key elements of the first phase have greatly exceeded what both the developer and the town anticipated. Utility line extensions, road widths, site design, and building development—all have been held to higher standards than would be required at a more level terrain. Whereas many of the codes and town construction specifications were written to meet the special demands of mountain construction, the town's standards never anticipated the requirements of a development of this magnitude. Meanwhile, the developer seems more interested in cutting costs than funding quality improvements as the project continues.
2. *Payment of "wholesale" improvements.* Early on, the town and the developer had to determine the shared cost, responsibility for improvements, and timing in the construction of necessary capital improvements. Under their initial agreement, the Far East Development Company was to pay the costs up front for wholesale improvements (e.g., pump stations, water tanks, water and wastewater mains serving the entire development), with the individual subdivisions paying for "retail" utility lines serving the individual properties. However, as the project proceeds, the developer continually demands that the town pay a greater portion of the cost of wholesale improvements, arguing those improvements benefit the entire town. The town board has recently agreed to subsidize some of the capital improvements.
3. *Outside project reviews.* Because of the regional impact of this development and the need to protect the natural habitat, the master development agreement required review by the Rosewood Forest Services, Army Corps of Engineers, and state highway department, not to mention several county agencies. Even though the developer knew about these reviews when it signed the master development agreement, its representatives now blame the staff for what they believe are excessive costs in meeting the requirements of these agencies. They have repeatedly stated their belief that "the town should pay for many of these requirements because of the benefit of this development to the town, rather than passing on all the costs of these requirements to the developer."
4. *Potential failure of the metropolitan financing district.* The town permitted the developer to establish a metropolitan taxing district that allowed the developer to tax the property in the development for needed infrastructure improvements. The tax district was intended to provide a financial buffer to the town and to allow the developer to recoup infrastructure costs from buyers in lieu of conventional financing. However, if this development fails, the tax burden on the

property in this metropolitan taxing district could delay further development of the property for many years to come. A failed property could also damage the credit rating of the Rosedale community.

5. *Discontinuation of Rosedale's free trash service.* The town's residents have enjoyed free trash service since incorporation, because the town pays the local trash company from general funds rather than by assessing residents a service fee. However, the cost to extend this service to the new development would be prohibitive, so the manager has recommended that the town discontinue this service to all residents. (Because the mayor works for the local trash disposal service, this issue may be difficult for him.)
6. *The need to balance development reviews and construction issues with other town priorities.* At the same time the development is being planned and constructed, the town board and staff have been juggling other projects including a major highway expansion, development in other parts of the town, construction of new businesses and homes to serve the new development, expansion of the wastewater plant to serve new growth, and finalizing plans for a new town hall.
7. *Tap fees.* The final issue is the question of when the developer should pay the cost of connecting homes in Sky Hawk Ridge to the town's water and sewer lines. Under the terms of the master development agreement, the developer was to pay tap fees for each phase up front. The town board has already agreed to allow the development to proceed without the payment of tap fees in the first phase of development, a decision in violation of the agreement. If it allows the developer to further delay payment of the tap fees to the end of the project, the town will need to "front end" the cost of these improvements and can only hope that it will be reimbursed at the final phase of construction. Because Far East Development Company submitted a clause (rejected by the town) that would have frozen the cost of the tap fees when the agreement was signed, staff are concerned that the developer will not be able to pay the cost of tap fees if the taps fees increase before the final phase of construction. In essence, not requiring payment on schedule will mean the town subsidizes the project, with a great deal of uncertainty about whether or not the developer will be able to pay the tap fees in the end.

Discussion Questions

1. If you were the in the shoes of Town Manager Kelly McGee, what would you recommend to the board regarding phase two of the proposed development?
2. If the project were abandoned, what would you suggest that the town board tell the members of the community who supported it? What would you tell those who opposed the project? What would you tell Winnie and the other old-timers?
3. Do you think it was in the long-term interest of the community to approve the project? Should staff have been more forceful in recommending delay of approvals for the development? Why or why not?
4. Should the town have allowed a metropolitan tax district to be formed to pay for infrastructure costs, or should the town have required the developer to pay these costs up front?
5. Was it unethical to let the developer pay costs for the town attorney and consultants? (This is a common practice to reduce the staff costs to towns for these extensive types of agreements.) What would have been an alternative?

6. Should the town assist the developer in paying for more of the wholesale improvements because the town benefits by the construction of these improvements? Where should it strike a balance between subsidizing economic development and requiring developers to pay the cost of improvements that benefit their development?
7. How should McGee and the staff have handled the public comments about "heads rolling" due to pressure from the developer?
8. Should these types of projects be delayed until staff is fully comfortable with their compliance to town standards, especially given the impact of this type of development on the region?
9. To save the project for the long term, should the town relax some of the initial standards for construction?
10. Should the town board and staff have looked for better ways to involve the long-term residents in the planning process? Is changing the nature of the community to a resort community in the long-term interest of the town?
11. Should the town manager and staff have confronted the developer early in the project about unethical behavior associated with the dinner and up-front demands for concessions?

Suggested Simulation Roles

Town board members
Town manager
Far East representative(s)
Town attorney
Staff (finance, planning, public works)
Water and sewer consultant
Finance consultant
Anti-development community members
Pro-development community members
Small business or construction firm owner
New property owner
Environmentalists
Government representatives (U.S. Forest Service, BLM)
The widow Winnie and other old-timers

9

The Chief versus the Council Member

June S. Speakman

Background

A community of 19,500 residents, Brookton is a short commute from a small Northeastern city and a reasonable commute from several other large urban centers. Its residents are primarily professionals, many of whom have moved to town for the excellent schools, the beauty of the place, and its high quality of life. Crime is low, trees and parks are plentiful, water sports and golf abound, and the small retail district meets the residents' daily needs.

As in many similar upscale communities, the populace leans to the Republican Party, although its location in New England adds social liberalism to Brookton's political climate. Town government is lean, with most local tax dollars going to the schools. The council-manager form of government generally serves the community well: despite partisan elections, residents expect high-quality services in a minimally political environment. In recent years, there has been a strong antitax movement in town that manifests itself at summer town meetings on finances.

The town manager, Paul Hathaway, has been on the job for just six months. Prior to his appointment by the town council, he had served as director of Brookton's department of public works for twenty years. A native of the town, he was popular with the residents and familiar to the council. He was appointed after the council summarily dismissed his predecessor, Harry Franks, whose dozen years of service were marked by an increasing hostility to the town council.

The episode that led to Franks's dismissal involved his loyalty to an unpopular and ineffective fire chief. Council members frequently bore the brunt of citizens' complaints about the chief. In turn, Franks resented council comments about his department managers—in fact, he was openly disdainful of their public comments about the fire service. At the council meeting immediately preceding his dismissal, Franks had rolled his eyes, laughed out loud, and refused to answer a variety of questions from the council. Hathaway, the new manager, had observed this dynamic both from his perch at the department of public works and from his seat in the audience at council meetings.

Also attending these meetings was Brookton's new police chief, Jack Forester, who had been hired by Franks six months prior to Franks's departure. Forester was a consummate professional and had recently retired from a stellar career with the state police. During his hiring interviews, Franks had made clear to Forester his disrespect for the "politicians" on the council and had given him tips on how to minimize their "meddling" in department affairs. Hathaway was an unknown quantity to Police Chief Forester, but Forester did know that he could be summarily dismissed by the manager and that the manager in turn could be summarily dismissed by the council.

Brookton's five-member town council consisted of four Republicans and one Democrat. Two of these members had been elected six months earlier—one was the lone Democrat and the other was the former police chief. The former chief, Nate Donardo, had run the police department for a dozen years, using a management style that was relaxed and casual. He had a close relationship with his officers, many of whom he still saw at the local coffee shop. The Democrat, Alicia Simmons, was a college professor in political science and card-carrying member of the American Civil Liberties Union. She had run for office at the request of the local Democratic Party and frequently acted in a manner that indicated that she was driven more by ideology than by a desire to please voters.

The Case

Upon arriving in Brookton, Chief Forester found a department in a brand new, state-of-the-art facility. However, he discovered that it operated under half-century-old personnel policies and an unwritten but uncontested code of conduct. As he understood it, this code was unprofessional and potentially dangerous. Forester saw the relaxed dress, casual demeanor, and flexible work rules of the department as problematic from the perspectives of both esprit de corps and law enforcement. His career as a state trooper had imbued him with the belief that officers, by both appearance and demeanor, must command respect and convey authority.

The officers, however, had a different perspective: one cultivated by their former boss, now-Councilman Donardo. Like many of them, he was born and raised in Brookton. He practiced a community policing philosophy before it was called that. Officers should, in his view, spend time at the local coffee shop, learn the names and problems of the local teenagers, and be familiar with particular difficult family situations. Decorum, procedures, and sharp dress were less important, and there was little emphasis on familiarity with current investigatory techniques and data analysis.

Once on the job, Chief Forester discovered that he had inherited a loose assortment of practices, policies, and rules that seemed anything but definitive. Therefore, consistent with his plan to modernize and professionalize the department, one of his first acts was to draft a forty-page "Manual of Police Policies and Procedures." Its contents were inspired and informed both by the chief's experience in the state police and by his study of similar codes in numerous other local police departments.

Forester organized the manual to factor in the existing guidelines (such as he could find them) while adding more definitive sections on leadership, professional conduct and courtesy, personal appearance, use of alcohol off duty, gambling, meal breaks, saluting, telephone usage, use of tobacco and chewing gum, and outside associations. The part about outside associations had two features: it prohibited officers from associating with individuals with a criminal past, and it required them to obtain the chief's approval before joining any outside club or organization.

The chief believed these new rules would bring his department into the twenty-first century and protect the town against liability. Implementation of these rules—as now presented in the manual—was contingent on approval by the town council, which typically looked to the town manager and town solicitor for advice on such matters. The chief had submitted the draft manual to the former town manager, Harry Franks, and had had it reviewed by the town's lawyer, but had not yet submitted it to the town council when Hathaway came on board. Four months into Hathaway's tenure, Forester presented his manual to Hathaway.

Hathaway faced a dilemma. He doubted the feasibility of Forester's proposed manual and considered sharing his misgivings with the town council. He knew all the police officers, having attended high school with several of them, and during his tenure at the department of public works, he had worked well with them on a number of projects. Given his understanding of the culture of the town's police department, he knew that the newest policies and procedures that Forester developed for the manual would be unwelcome.

In addition, having witnessed the town council's public, rancorous confrontation with his predecessor, Hathaway understood the council's frame of mind. The two behaviors of Franks that had most frustrated the council were his steadfast support of his department heads in the face of council criticism and his tendency to withhold information. Hathaway did not want to give the council the impression that its concerns about any of his department heads were irrelevant or inappropriate—nor did he want the council to lose trust in him. During his job interview with the council for the town manager position, two of his selling points were his commitment to open government and his acknowledgment that he served at the pleasure of the council. To keep his job, Hathaway had to keep the council's trust and assure its members that he took their concerns seriously.

Privately, Town Manager Hathaway knew that he was not an expert in police procedures. Regardless, he was loath to provoke a confrontation with Chief Forester. In his former position heading the department of public works, Hathaway had sat next to Forester at the weekly manager's meetings. There, they heard Franks (then town manager) repeatedly denigrate the town council, and Franks also was widely known to prompt the department heads to disregard council members' meddling in administrative affairs.

Hathaway was unsure if Forester shared Franks's attitudes; however, he could see that Forester was clearly having difficulty transitioning from the very professional, almost paramilitary state police organization to this small-town police department. Hathaway's first act as town manager had been to fire the fire chief, who had been the primary bone of contention between Franks and the council. Now fire department morale was at rock bottom, and contract negotiations were looming. The last thing Hathaway needed was an unhappy police chief managing an unhappy police department.

Keeping his reservations to himself for the time being, Town Manager Hathaway put the proposed manual on the July council agenda. If the council approved the proposed rules and regulations, he reasoned, problem solved. The chief gets what he wants, Hathaway has no conflicts to mediate, and the council goes on to the next issue.

However, that was not going to happen, at least not right away.

The five council members first learned of the proposed rule changes when they received their packets on the Wednesday prior to the Monday meeting. Attached to the forty-page "Manual of Police Policies and Procedures" was Hathaway's one-sentence recommendation that the manual be adopted as presented.

In the remaining few days prior to the council meeting, council members began getting calls and visits from two sources: rank-and-file police officers and the ACLU. The first, who insisted on anonymity during their calls and meetings, complained about the chief's proposed rules, asking "Why is he fixing what isn't broken?" and "Doesn't he know this isn't the state police?" Some of the officers said, "He doesn't understand how to run a small-town department," and "We won't be able to get our job done under these rules."

The ACLU had a different set of concerns, and the Friday before the meeting it articulated them in long letter to each of the council members. According to the ACLU, several provisions in the proposed manual contained unconstitutional constraints on officers' personal freedoms. The ACLU promised to assist any officers who believed their constitutional rights were being violated by the new policies and procedures.

Among the offending policies and procedures were:

- A prohibition on publicly criticizing the police department
- A prohibition against on-duty and off-duty conduct that "brings or may bring the department into disrepute," such as profanity, immoral conduct, and intoxication
- A requirement that officers not join any group that is deemed by the police chief "to be detrimental to the force"
- A requirement that police officers "discontinue relationships with people who are under investigation or have a reputation in the community"
- A prohibition against "engaging in idle conversation" while on duty.

The Council Meeting

At that Monday meeting in July, several off-duty officers were in the audience as well as a representative of the ACLU. Chief Forester presented the proposed "Manual of Police Policies and Procedures" to the council. The manager and town solicitor recommended that the manual be adopted as proposed. The ACLU representative then rose to present her organization's objections to the proposal, and the council began its questioning.

It was clear from the start that the four Republican council members including former Police Chief Donardo would vote to support Chief Forester. Councilwoman Simmons, however, was another story. She indicated that she had spent some time in conversation with the ACLU and also that her training as a political scientist gave her some background in constitutional matters.

Simmons asked the town solicitor whether he had researched the constitutionality of the policies in the manual that concerned political associations and public criticism. She suggested that were the manual adopted as written, the town might leave itself open to lawsuits, and she reminded her fellow council members that constitutional challenges were often lengthy and very costly.

Simmons also asked the town manager if he had considered the impact of the rules changes on police department morale, especially in light of the situation with the fire service. She clearly was not about to defer to the chief's expertise, the town solicitor's advice, or the town manager's recommendations. She reiterated her familiarity with constitutional law, and her mention of potentially high legal fees made her Republican colleagues on the town council squirm. During her statement, Chief Forester became visibly irritated, while the off-duty officers sat silently.

In concluding her statement, Simmons requested a one-month delay of the council's vote so that she could further study the constitutional issues. The police chief rose in protest, claiming that the town's lawyer had fully reviewed the manual, that the state police had adopted almost identical guidelines, and that the police union had no objection to the new rules. The chief contended that adoption of these rules was essential if he were to move forward with his plans to bring the department into the twenty-first century. Former Chief Donardo looked displeased with the new chief's implied criticism of the Donardo-era police department. Simmons wondered aloud why so many officers had contacted her and why they insisted on anonymity.

Over the police chief's objections, the council voted to table its vote on the manual until the August meeting.

The Decision Problem

The next day, there were two messages waiting for Town Manager Hathaway when he came in from his morning run—from Police Chief Forester and Councilwoman Simmons. The chief asked to see him immediately. The chief walked into the manager's office in full dress uniform complete with crisply pressed pants, shiny badge, and sidearm. He remained standing, almost at attention, during the entire conversation.

The chief made clear to the manager that he could not manage a department as casual and unprofessional as Brookton's; that these policies and procedures were essential to his improvement plan for the department; and that he had several job offers outstanding, including one as chief of security at a corporation's national headquarters. Chief Forester said he believed Simmons was humiliating him at the previous night's council meeting and that he would not sit through such a circus again. "Get the council on board," were his departing words.

Hathaway dealt with Simmons's message by calling her university office. She told him she had two questions and a statement for him.

- *Question 1.* Was Hathaway aware of the degree of opposition to the new rules among the rank-and-file officers? Hathaway responded that the police union had approved the changes before they ever got to the town council. Simmons again wondered why, then, she was receiving so many calls. In fact, she said, one very senior patrol officer had shown up at her door and sat at her table for two hours reviewing the flaws in the chief's proposed manual. How could these rules be a good idea if they were so unpopular with the officers?
- *Question 2.* Did the town solicitor understand the constitutional questions at stake? His unconditional support for the chief's proposal seemed odd to Simmons. Clearly the provisions about privileged speech and freedom of association were violations of the First Amendment. Why did the solicitor not object to these?
- *Statement.* While Simmons acknowledged that the other council members seemed not to share her concerns, she nevertheless made clear to Hathaway that she would oppose the new policies and procedures manual if it went forward with the problem provisions. She further warned him to be prepared for additional statements by herself and the ACLU at the next meeting. She added that she would not hesitate to use the local newspaper to communicate with the voters on the issue. Last, she warned Hathaway that she intended to remind her colleagues on the council—in public if necessary—of their recent difficulties with the former fire chief and town manager.

"Get the chief to change those rules," were her final words.

For Hathaway as the town manager, the challenge was this: how to keep the police chief happy without provoking a confrontation with the council. Could he navigate the choppy waters dividing a competent, ambitious, sought-after police chief and a riled-up councilmember and her ACLU allies?

Discussion Questions

1. Given his concerns about the new rules, should Town Manager Hathaway defer to Police Chief Forester and hope that at least three council members will vote for the new manual at the August meeting?
2. Should Hathaway encourage the police chief to consider changing the offending provisions of the manual? If so, how might he do this?

3. Is there a way for Hathaway to persuade Councilwoman Simmons to go along with the policy and procedure changes as contained in the manual?
4. What might Hathaway have done to avoid the public confrontation between Simmons and the police chief at the July town council meeting?
5. What might the police chief have done to minimize opposition to his proposed rule changes?
6. Should Hathaway be proactive in working with the media to build support for the chief?
7. Should the police department implement a policy that prohibits officers from contacting council members?
8. Is there an alternative means for modernizing and professionalizing the police department without extensive written rules?

Suggested Simulation Roles

Paul Hathaway, town manager
Jack Forester, police chief
Alicia Simmons, council member
ACLU representative
Police union president

Scenario

The town manager convenes a meeting to resolve the issues arising at the July town council meeting. His goal is to fend off a confrontation at the August meeting by finding common ground.

The simulation asks students to develop a position for each role. During the simulation, participants advocate for their position as the town manager attempts to achieve consensus. After 30 minutes, participants and observers analyze the outcome of the simulated meeting and present alternative approaches for each role.

Part IV

Promoting the Community's Future

Introduction to Part IV

Promoting the Community's Future

Planning is a process, not a document, so it is important to remember that it must involve citizens in appropriate ways. But exactly how and when varies greatly, especially since strategic planning is considered a top-down activity. Because planning often focuses on economic development, it inevitably causes some clash between tradition and change.

Planning is always controversial, whether employing the traditional type, which focuses on land use, or the strategic type, which focuses on changing the community in fundamental ways.

Land-use planning is typically long range, involving a span of twenty to twenty-five years. It takes time to find ways to finance building infrastructure, entice private developers, and attract business and industry to the community. This gives the community the opportunity to involve citizens in focus groups, public hearings, and planning meetings. Thus, a community that is trying, for example, to plot the future of a recent annexation of 3,000 acres of farmland will employ land-use planning.

Strategic planning is short term, often five or fewer years out. It involves setting goals and objectives that can be accomplished in a limited time frame even as they will fundamentally affect a community. Strategic planning may encompass some elements of land-use planning but often focuses on even larger issues: whether to grow, whether to merge a city and county, whether to change the form of government. It always requires the organization to take a hard, honest look at its present strengths and weaknesses, identify possible opportunities, and single out what actions might be perceived as threatening by the community. For example, a community may have abundant water but a poor network of roads. Too, it possibly could attract industries that could use its resources—but with the corresponding possibility of threats to the quality of those resources.

Economic planning can cut across both land-use planning and strategic planning. Often strategic planning focuses on how to help the community expand its economic base as well as determine what must be done to provide an environment that will attract business investment and promote the growth of existing commercial establishments. The answers lie not only in how land will be used but also in organizational effectiveness, intergovernmental relations, and the sophistication of communication and transportation networks.

Case 10, "Conflict and Cooperation," demonstrates the complexities of development when multiple jurisdictions are involved and there are significant environmental issues. The institutional actors include cities, counties, an airport, and multiple federal agencies. They must grapple with such questions as: How can open space and airport needs be protected and smart growth be implemented? How can the diverse interests of farmers, environmentalists, and property developers be reconciled? The outcome will significantly affect economic development in the area.

Case 11, "Race, Politics, and Low-income Housing," seeks to resolve the seeming conflict of providing adequate low-income housing while finding space for a medical school to expand rather than leave the community. The medical school is a major employer but must have room to expand; it also has an attractive offer to move to the city where the state's flagship university is located. The city has a need for low-income housing, but the only expansion space available for the medical school involves razing an affordable-housing complex. The manager thus must reconcile the needs of a mostly white medical school with the needs of primarily African-American low-income residents, while making sure the community as a whole protects valuable cultural and economic assets. One interesting aspect of the case is the political burden placed on the manager to find a solution.

The two cases in Part IV allow the reader to analyze decisions involving a number of management practices. These include policy facilitation; citizen service; performance measurement; initiative, risk taking, vision, creativity, and innovation; democratic advocacy and citizen participation; diversity; strategic planning; advocacy and interpersonal communication; and media relations.

10

Conflict and Cooperation

Leighann Moffitt and Julie Car

Background

This case explores a county manager's options for development and open-space preservation in a complex political and regulatory setting—currently an agricultural area. Property owners and elected officials are anxious to allow urban uses. However, environmental regulations require portions of the area to be committed to open space and agriculture, and the area lacks adequate flood protection. The county manager must chart a course that protects both the environment and the residents while addressing the concerns of the elected officials. Events have come to a head in the month of May.

The three key jurisdictions in this case study are Rural County North (County North), Urban County South (County South), and Downtown City (the city). The key individuals involved are the manager of Urban County South (the county manager), the manager of Downtown City (the city manager), three representatives of development interests (the land-use attorney, the retired public manager, and the developer representative, collectively known as the landowner team), two representative developers (the prominent family developer and the individualist developer), and the farmer.

The area being considered for urbanization is within what is called the Basin, with a large river along the west side and a large drainage canal to the east. The levee system that protects the basin from flooding has been decertified by the U.S. Army Corps of Engineers because it does not provide 100-year flood protection. The 53,000-acre Basin is split approximately in half by the two counties. The northern portion of Downtown City also falls within the Basin and includes an established urban area surrounded by huge swaths of new subdivisions built over the past five years.

The Basin contains a large international airport that is operated by County South and requires appropriate buffering for noise and safety. North-south and east-west interstate highways run through the Basin, giving the area excellent regional freeway access. The only other infrastructure consists of agricultural drainage, irrigation canals, and farm roads. Agriculture still dominates, particularly in the north and around the airport, but urban encroachment and high costs are placing significant pressures on farms. Any new development would require extensive infrastructure for municipal services.

Figure 1 Map of the Basin

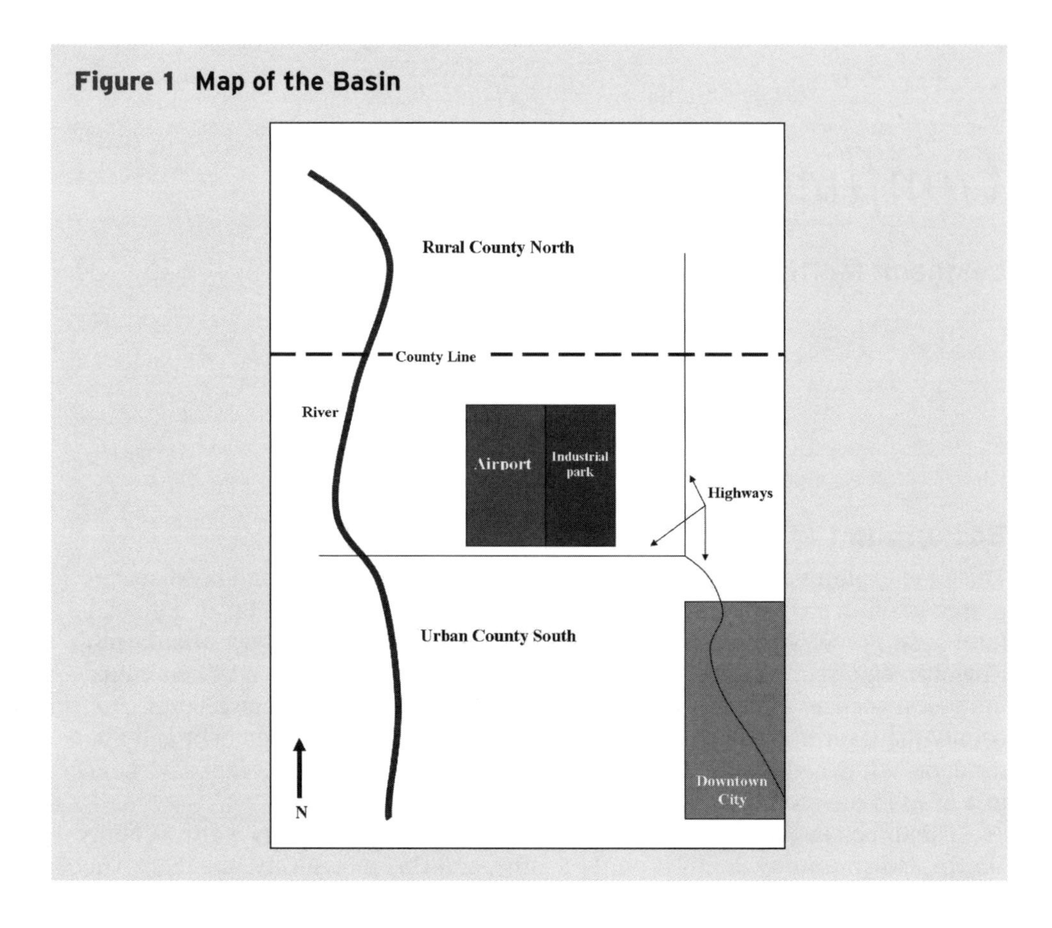

The Case

About six years ago, Downtown City and County South signed a memorandum of understanding (MOU), agreeing to pursue additional urbanization in the unincorporated portion of the Basin in County South. The two jurisdictions would share any revenues generated. The MOU called for Downtown City to annex and urbanize some portion of the Basin, while County South would retain the open space and agricultural lands. County South would continue to control both the airport and a large, adjacent industrial and office area that had yet to attract new business development. Key MOU principles involved the preservation of open space, airport protection, and smart-growth design.

The MOU seemed a breakthrough at the time, with city and county staff cooperating with each other and coordinating planning. Cooperation was important to the respective managers because residents of Downtown City and County South tend to band together on regional issues. However, the MOU did not identify the actual location of development. Many landowners do not want their property included in the area that must remain in open space and agriculture. Because of this, the elected officials of County South requested a study that would identify areas that should remain in open space as well as the financial mechanisms for implementing the preservation strategy.

The Issues

The Regional Context

County North, population 78,000, has plans to develop 7,500 acres in the southern end of its jurisdiction, within the Basin and adjacent to the area under consideration in County South. County North is relatively poor and has identified urban uses as essential for its long-term economic viability. County South, population 562,000, and Downtown City, population 468,000, also view the Basin as a logical place to develop, but are planning for urbanization to occur in County South.

A developing industrial park next to the airport in County South is designed to serve as a regional employment center, with the airport and major north-south and east-west highways providing easy access. County South and Downtown City anticipate an increase in retail revenue because of the projected increase in population due to this industrial park, and they want to capitalize on it by developing before County North can. Smaller suburban cities in the region have built positive revenue by generating retail and employment uses.

However, with the downturn in the housing market, development interests in the three jurisdictions are working to ensure that their respective areas are positioned to take advantage of a future market turnaround.

Levees and Flood Protection

Existing levees had been improved and certified for 100-year flood protection, which allowed for urbanization for 70,000+ residents within the Downtown City portion of the Basin. However, the levees were decertified by the U.S. Army Corps of Engineers after Hurricane Katrina. The potential depth of flooding in some parts of the Basin approaches 30 feet. The Federal Emergency Management Agency, which recently gave the Basin a preliminary designation as a "special flood hazard zone," is remapping the Basin and will have an official designation in December. The preliminary designation restricts new development, including civic and commercial buildings, until 100-year flood protection is achieved.

The local flood control agency is embarking on a major levee improvement project to provide 100-year protection within two years and 200-year protection within five years. This project is a high priority for all the jurisdictions, and progress toward both regulatory approvals and actual construction is proceeding at a rapid pace. Improvements are expected to begin within the year.

Although all parties agree that opening up new urban areas cannot occur until the levee project is finished, they view additional development as a potential source of funding for the necessary levee improvements. Therefore, planning for urbanization now will allow jurisdictions to be ready for development upon levee certification.

Endangered Species Act Requirements and the Habitat Conservation Plan

The Basin serves as a habitat for a variety of endangered species. Under the Endangered Species Act, a habitat conservation plan (HCP) is required to mitigate the expected loss of habitat and the resulting "take" of species by urban development. Upon adoption of an HCP, the federal wildlife agency issues an "incidental take permit" to allow a specified amount of development. Fifteen years ago, Downtown City and County North were signatories to an HCP that permits the development of 17,500 acres in the Basin. County South did not sign the HCP: at the time it was generally assumed that unincorporated County South land would remain in agriculture.

The habitat conservation plan covers twenty-two species, but the two flagship species are the Swainson's hawk and the giant garter snake. The hawk nests in trees along the river and forages in farmlands both inside the Basin and on the other side of the river (outside the Basin). The snake depends the most on the Basin's agricultural irrigation and drainage canals.

A local conservancy, which is a key landowner in the area, was created to manage the implementation of the HCP. The HCP requires the conservancy to ensure ongoing farming of much of its property. Thus the conservancy faces many of the same pressures with economically viable agricultural practices as the farming interests face.

Three lawsuits against Downtown City, County South, and the federal wildlife agency have challenged the validity of the HCP's mitigation measures. The environmental community believes that the jurisdictions do not do enough to offset the impact of development. During the final ruling that validated the most recent HCP, the judge indicated that it would be difficult to permit additional development beyond the 17,500 acres covered by the HCP. Furthermore, environmentalists have rallied against the MOU because it allows for the study of additional growth. Since the entire Basin is considered as habitat under the HCP, any development not currently covered by the existing HCP will need a new HCP to prove that the effects are not detrimental to the species.

The managers of the airport expansion and flood control projects are working to develop separate habitat mitigation efforts to offset the effects of their projects. The flood control project in particular has the potential to remove significant riparian areas and change the underlying assumptions of the current HCP. However, the flood control agency is working closely with the wildlife agencies to design measures to improve existing habitats—measures such as connecting canals and planting replacement trees.

Open-space Study

Downtown City and County South engaged a consultant for an open-space study to determine which areas within County South are most suitable for urbanization and which areas have the highest value for open space. The open-space study was expected to analyze the issues raised over the costs of the long-term preservation of open space and habitat. In the end, lack of a clear pattern and pressures from development and environmental interests made it difficult for the study to definitively conclude where growth should occur and where land should be left undeveloped.

Both interest groups opposed adopting the study. The development interests were concerned that it did not factor in either the proximity of existing urban services or the feasibility of providing them in future. The environmental interests were concerned about the accuracy and reliability of the biological data used in the study. In the end, the completed study contained conceptual open-space configurations, and plans are to use it as background data for identifying areas for urban growth and mechanisms to finance open-space preservation.

The Airport

Managed by County South, the airport is important to the region for both its transportation and economic benefits. County South has recently adopted a master plan allowing its expansion. The Federal Aviation Administration requires all airports to control "bird strikes" around the runways. Since the airport is located in the Pacific Flyway—a major path for migratory birds—staff has developed management plans to minimize the presence of waterfowl on adjacent airport-owned land.

This limitation was not anticipated by the adopted habitat conservation plan, however. The amount of land taken up by the airport and the potential restrictions on habitat will likely be a factor in negotiating a new HCP required to permit the expansion as well as any future private development.

Agricultural Water

Agricultural water in County South is provided by a private agricultural water company. As farmers fallow their land in anticipation of development, the water costs increase for the remaining farmers. These costs also affect the local conservancy's ability to maintain habitat for the HCP. The giant garter snake requires a system of active agricultural canals, while the hawk relies on agricultural activities for foraging.

The Stakeholders

County South

County South provides urban services to a large population and has the capacity to serve this new community. However, the premise of the negotiated joint-planning MOU is that the creation of a long-term sustainable community is best served if the city provides urban services. The elected officials of County South are frustrated with the lack of progress toward a plan for urbanization. To ensure progress is being made, the officials require regular reports from the county manager.

At the urging of development interests, some elected officials of County South have investigated whether it might be in the county's best interests to pursue development on its own rather than to continue to work with Downtown City. Therefore, although the development process is being led by the staff of the city, the county manager is under pressure to demonstrate progress.

The County South Manager

The County South manager is a career government manager with many years in county government. Two of his key objectives are preserving open space (as desirable for quality of life) and ensuring that the county remains in good fiscal health. The second is becoming increasingly difficult.

Downtown City

The immediate issue for Downtown City is the lack of adequate flood protection for residents of the Basin. FEMA's preliminary designation of a special flood hazard zone effectively imposes a moratorium on new construction within the already urbanized area of the Basin, including public service facilities such as libraries and fire stations. The official designation in December will most likely require residents to obtain flood insurance until the levee is built. Many citizens are outraged by this, so the city's elected officials are not focused on opening up additional lands in the Basin for development.

The City Manager

Also possessing many years of experience, the Downtown City manager was hired from another jurisdiction to revitalize the city and promote business-friendly practices. The city manager has been widely praised for promoting positive growth within the city. Although the city and county managers have a respectful working relationship, the pressures for County South to break from the MOU could hamper their future cooperation.

County North

The adopted habitat conservation plan allows County North to develop land immediately adjacent to County South. County North is concerned that additional Basin development by County South and Downtown City will undermine the HCP it shares with the city and result in the federal wildlife agency revoking the incidental take permit that allows for the implementation of County South's development plan. The HCP requires that mitigation land be acquired within the Basin, further limiting the supply of land for other uses. Any additional development proposed by Downtown City and County South would also require mitigation, and that may greatly affect the price and availability of mitigation land within the Basin.

Development Interests

GREEDY DEVELOPERS PUSHING FORWARD

Developers have acquired land in several locations within County South. County South elected officials are being pressured to accept and process two urban development applications separate from the MOU. (Environmental studies and land-use plans would need to be completed before the applications could be approved.) These applications for County South–led development are being used by developers to pressure the city to move forward with the MOU-required joint planning process in a timely manner.

Several developers' representatives have advocated for a larger role in the process. One of these developers comes from a prominent area family and has strong political ties within the region. The other developer, more of an individualist, wants to develop a portion of the area that has good potential for urban development because of freeway access, existing infrastructure, and its close proximity to the city. However, the wildlife regulatory agencies have also designated this land as an important habitat area. Anxious to develop their land, both developers have retained the services of the local land-use attorney (described below), who regularly pleads their cases to County South's elected officials at public meetings.

Recently, three developer representatives have banded together to represent the interests of many of the landowners in the unincorporated area. Referred to as the "landowner team," they include the local land use attorney, a retired public agency manager, and a developer representative. All three have good relationships with the county manager, the city manager, city and county elected officials, and other parties involved in the development process. The landowner team is coming off a recent success in which it acted as the development team for a large regional project in County South. This team focuses on generating consensus among the landowners and acts as a liaison with the city and county staff. Ultimately, a working group representing all interests (farming, development, and environmental) will create a land-use plan for the area.

Farming Interests

A small but vocal group of farmers in County South is claiming that agriculture is no longer economically viable in the area and, further, that any attempt to designate land as permanent open space would lead to the financial ruin of the farmer. They assert that because of the land's proximity to urban services and its relatively short distance to the downtown core, they should be allowed to develop. Pressures from nearby subdivisions are also causing problems for farmers, including their inability to move farm equipment from one field to another because of urban traffic on formerly rural roads; the high cost of agricultural water, partly due to high pumping costs; complaints from urban residents about odors, dust, and the aerial application of pesticides; and encroachment on and vandalism of farm property and equipment. Protecting the economic interests of these agricultural property owners is a key interest of one County South elected official.

However, a portion of this agricultural land is in a Swainson's hawk protection zone. The wildlife regulatory agencies said in the adopted habitat conservation plan that the land was essential to the survival of the hawk. Because County South did not sign the HCP, the farmers assert that they should not be held to the restrictions of the plan. Therefore, they are pressuring County South elected officials to consider their land for urban development, potentially by moving forward in disregard of the MOU and taking the lead on development or by attempting to pressure Downtown City to include this land in the annexation area.

CONFLICTING INTERESTS
REGIONAL REGULATION
PURPOSE (LAND USE) TIMEFRAMES

INSUFFICIENT RESOURES/INFRASTRUCTURE TO SUPPORT RESIDENTS

Environmental Interests

Over the past thirty years, the local environmental community has filed numerous lawsuits over urbanization issues within the area, and more are expected. As stated before, the habitat conservation plan was litigated three times, at great expense to the federal wildlife agency, Downtown City, and County North. The local environmental community supports the recorded judge's opinion: it would be difficult if not impossible to prove that development exceeding what the HCP allows will *not* jeopardize the listed species. They actively oppose Downtown City and County South's planning efforts for the area and have stated that any land-use plan will be litigated.

The state and federal wildlife regulatory agencies are concerned about the effect of additional development on certain species. City and County South staff have been actively working with the agencies to develop a preservation plan to complement the conservation efforts of the HCP and not undermine the agencies which, in turn, have been receptive to continuing dialogue and see an opportunity to improve on the success of the HCP.

Community Residents

In addition to recent concerns about adequate flood protection, residents of the large new housing tracts built in the last five years within the city portion of the Basin are unhappy about the city's lack of services in their new area. At public hearings they ask the city to build the public facilities promised to them before moving on to the next project.

The Decision Problem

A majority of the elected officials of County South are frustrated with the lack of progress over the past six years. Now they are insisting on urbanization of a portion of the area and resolution of the challenges associated with open space and agricultural preservation. Although the city's elected officials are making some progress toward urbanization, the complex issues have caused the project to proceed slowly. For the city, annexing additional areas for urbanization is on a back burner due to both the decertification of the levees and the recent FEMA designation limiting all development, including civic and commercial uses.

At a recent public meeting, the elected officials of County South asked whether the county should undertake urbanization separately from the city. The officials hope that the results of an open-space study will definitively answer the question of where urbanization should, and should not, occur as well as give recommendations on funding that open space. Unfortunately, the complexity of the issues—habitat preservation, airport protection, and development pressure, to name just a few—affect the entire area, so it is difficult to conclude that one area is better suited for open space than another. At their last public meeting, County South elected officials agreed that the MOU jurisdictional roles identifying the city as the agent of development and County South as the agent of open space no longer apply. City and County South officials wish to be equally engaged in both areas. The county manager has two obvious options to recommend: either that the county stay the course or go it alone. However, less-obvious options are likely to surface amid the large number of concerned parties and the charged political atmosphere.

County South may opt to continue to work with the city manager to eventually annex the area and accrue shared tax revenue. The county manager sees some benefit to this approach, including retaining the county's valued working relationship with the city; sharing in revenues from retail and employment land uses without the cost of providing urban services; and sharing the costs and challenges of potential litigation. This approach, however, is not without problems. Downtown City has not addressed the elected officials' concern that it (the city) is not truly committed to development within the area; the location and form of urban growth remains undecided; and thus far there are no financial mechanisms for fairly and equitably implementing a preservation strategy.

Conversely, County South may choose to break from the negotiated memorandum of understanding and take the lead on urbanizing the area. If so, it could realize all, not just part, of the tax revenue benefits from development. By doing this, the county itself could shape the type and location of the new development, could retain all revenue from the area, and could proceed with necessary long-range planning while bypassing the city's issues with its residents. But there are three obvious problems with this approach, too: it will strain the relationship with the city manager; it will affect County South's budget for infrastructure construction; and, for violating the HCP, it will make County South vulnerable to litigation from environmental interests, the city, and County North.

Discussion Questions

1. Should the manager of County South recommend to the elected officials (a) that the county break from the MOU with the city or (b) that it retain the MOU, under which Downtown City will lead the urban development process?
2. If County South retains the MOU, how does the county manager address the elected officials' concerns about timely progress, given that the city is leading the effort?
3. What approach should the County South manager suggest to eventually resolve where development should occur?
4. Farm property owners view a decision about what area is allowed to urbanize as "winners versus losers." Should this perspective play a factor in the ultimate decision-making process? Should the two managers work to achieve economic parity between those landowners that ultimately are allowed to develop? Should the public sector be involved in managing any system that seeks to compensate landowners who may not be allowed to develop, or should the private market address this issue?
5. Should the city or county elected officials even be working on urbanization before the flood-control issues are resolved?

Suggested Simulation Roles

Manager, Urban County South
Manager, Downtown City
Land-use attorney
Retired public manager
Representative of developer
Farmer
Member of the local environmental community
Landowner with development interests

11

Race, Politics, and Low-income Housing

Saundra Reinke

City Administrator Ford Thompson has a major crisis on his hands. The state's medical school, a major employer in the city, is under pressure to expand to a new satellite location in another part of the state. To keep the school in town, Thompson worked out a plan to sell the medical school a large public-housing project so it could have the land to expand. That plan has now become the centerpiece of a prominent racial controversy.

Background

With a population of about 250,000, Old Town has the amenities of many larger communities but the comfortable feel of a family-friendly, smaller town. The city's major employers are a federal nuclear facility, a military base, and a health-care community. The city hosts the state's only public medical school, along with a large Veterans Affairs hospital and three other major hospitals. The medical school benefits the community because it attracts highly paid professionals into the community, provides many well-paying jobs, and brings in a significant amount of research funding. The only major private industry is a series of chemical plants on the southeast side of the city.

Old Town is a classic Southern city with a rich history. The city has a well-kept historic district, featuring many homes that are more than 100 years old. Historical figures include a signer of the Declaration of Independence and a number of well-known Confederate leaders. Old Town's traditionally white population dominates its political and business elite, and the mayor is from one of Old Town's most prominent white families.

Old Town has another history, one that runs parallel with the dominant version. The city also contains the oldest, continuously operating black church in the nation. Old Town's proud black community has produced famous singers, educators, and ministers. Through the years of slavery, followed by segregation, the black community held tight. Many in the community can recall the race riot in 1970 and the day schools finally became integrated in 1972.

Beginning in the 1970s, members of the black community gradually began assuming leadership roles. At the same time, white families began moving out into surrounding suburban communities. As of the last census, about 60 percent of the city's population is black. With the population shift, Old Town found itself rife with problems common to large cities: poverty, crime, unemployment, and one of the worst public education systems in the state. These problems primarily affected blacks.

White flight contributed to the fiscal crisis that hit Old Town in the early 1990s, as real estate values fell and the tax base declined. At the same time, the demand for law enforcement and social services increased in step with Old Town's growing problems. The budget crisis prompted the city to take a drastic step: it consolidated with the surrounding county. Because the city was primarily black and the county was primarily white, the decision to consolidate was controversial. Black leaders were concerned that consolidation would weaken their political power and dilute black voting strength.

The eventual solution was to create commission districts, through gerrymandering, to produce racial equality on the commission. The mayor, to be elected at large and presumably to be determined by the white majority vote, would have little political power.

As a result, Old Town has a ten-member elected commission, a mayor, and a professional city administrator who reports to the commission. Today, five of the city's ten elected commissioners are black; five are white. Race remains a major issue in city politics: commissioners typically vote along racial lines. Commission meetings often run late while members argue and even swap public insults. In short, politics in Old Town is marked by conflict, not cooperation. And that conflict, whether explicitly or implicitly, centers on race.

The energetic young mayor, in office only a year, campaigned on a platform of progress and racial harmony. True to the abovementioned arrangement, the mayor has little power. He appoints individuals to certain influential boards, including the local housing authority, but votes at commission meetings only to break a tie.

City Administrator Ford Thompson is relatively new to town. He began his career in law enforcement, working his way up to a police chief position before moving on to a state-level position in law enforcement. From there, he took his first city administration job, coming to Old Town as the assistant city administrator.

The previous city administrator left eighteen months ago for a similar position in a larger city. But Thompson knows that his predecessor did not leave simply for the salary and prestige that come with managing a larger city. He left because he was fed up with local politics. Commissioners frequently bypassed the administrator, working directly with department heads. And the commission retained hiring and firing authority, leaving Thompson's predecessor frustrated. Moreover, the previous administrator was often caught in the cross fire between commissioners and despaired of their ever cooperating to improve government services.

This would be a difficult environment even for a seasoned administrator, but Thompson quickly demonstrated that he was a thoughtful listener and a tough but fair leader. He has carefully stayed in the background, letting elected officials take the credit when things go well. Since he is white, he has worked especially hard to build relationships with the black commissioners, although with limited success. Thompson has survived his rookie days as a city administrator, true, but he never forgets that he is just six votes away from the unemployment line.

The Case

About eighteen months ago (around the time the previous city administrator left), rumors began to fly concerning the state's medical school in Old Town. Like many medical schools in the nation, it faces intense pressure from the state to produce more doctors and nurses. However, the school is landlocked. Across the street to the west is a historically black college. On the north side is a large Veterans Affairs hospital. To the east and the south sits the city's largest low-income housing project, Graves Manor. There simply is no room to expand.

Consequently, the school's president began conversations with the president of the state's flagship university. The two schools had been cooperating on a number of research projects, so, for the two presidents, it seemed natural to begin discussing a medical school satellite in the same area as the flagship university. Located in a largely rural area, the flagship university's host community offered land that was comparatively cheap and easily bought. These conversations turned serious when a small military installation adjacent to the flagship university was ordered closed as part of the U.S. Defense Department's base realignment and closure (BRAC) process. The size of the property, its location adjacent to the flagship university, and the timing seemed perfect.

When the local press learned about it, the two presidents denied they had had any discussions, but in the face of aggressive local reporters and a deluge of questions from Old Town's political leaders, the two finally admitted they had been talking over the possibility of a satellite campus. Given the presidents' lack of candor, many of Old Town's leaders, black and white, concluded that they could not be trusted.

Suspecting that the two presidents might even be discussing moving the entire medical school out of Old Town, the local legislative delegation immediately went into action. The head of the local delegation, Representative Quincy Jones, and Senator James Black pushed through the state legislature a measure requiring a study of the expansion before either school proceeded. This law gave the delegation and the leadership of Old Town a year to work out a solution that would allow the medical school to expand in Old Town.

Clearly, keeping the medical school in town was critical to Old Town's future; thus, with the support of the local legislative delegation, the commission asked City Administrator Thompson to take the lead in finding the solution. He was eager to accept the challenge, genuinely believing that Old Town's economic future was tied to its medical community. Enlarging that community's size—and its ability to generate research funds—would create well-paying jobs the community desperately needed.

City Administrator Thompson saw only one practical, although not easy, solution: the medical school would have to purchase the Graves Manor property, home to some 900 individuals. Like all public-housing projects, Graves Manor operated under the direction of the Old Town Housing Authority (OTHA), an independent corporation under the supervision of the U.S. Department of Housing and Urban Development (HUD). OTHA is governed by a board whose members are appointed by the mayor. To make this solution work, the OTHA board would have to be persuaded to sell the Graves Manor property, HUD would have to approve the sale, the residents would need alternate housing, the medical school would have to be persuaded to purchase the property, and in all likelihood, Old Town would have to contribute financially to sweeten the purchase.

Thompson also knew he could not work on this solution on his own. To increase the chances of a successful outcome, he would need a committee including the major players. But he was leery of creating a large committee. His previous experience with committee work had taught him that committees must be kept small to be productive. Consequently, Thompson included a representative from the medical school, a representative from OTHA, and Old Town's budget director. All these individuals were white.

The committee quickly went to work and almost immediately concluded that Thompson's suggested solution (the purchase of Graves Manor) was the only viable one. Thereafter, the committee focused its attention on making that solution a reality. At the very first meeting, the OTHA representative noted that there were no black members of the committee and suggested the committee be expanded. He also asked about keeping the Graves Manor residents informed as well as the public at large.

Thompson disagreed on adding a black member since he planned to be in constant contact with the commission and legislative delegation, keeping them informed of the committee's work. He also indicated his preference for the committee to do its work quietly and with a minimum of publicity, to mitigate the reluctance of some community leaders to support the committee's solution.

Working quietly in the background over the course of the next six to seven months, City Administrator Thompson and his committee successfully convinced the OTHA board, local political leaders, HUD, and the medical school president that the best way to expand the medical school's capacity was for the school to purchase Graves Manor. Driven by the fear of losing the medical school, both black and white elected officials and community leaders united in support of Thompson's proposal.

Representative Jones and Senator Black (both black) were instrumental in convincing black political leaders to support Thompson's proposal. While no one tried to keep the solution a secret, neither did anyone take steps to inform the press or the public about the Graves Manor purchase. The paperwork to turn this solution into a reality was well on its way to completion when there was a major setback.

In this case, the setback took the form of a December 7 e-mail. Dave Brown, a member of the OTHA board, e-mailed a local property developer to encourage him to move ahead with building expensive condominiums in the downtown area. In addition to helping to revitalize the downtown, Brown noted that the development would tip the racial balance in that commission district (District 1) in favor of whites. (The departure of the approximately 900 Graves Manor residents, all black, plus the addition of some 200 white condominium owners would make District 1 a majority white district. The result might be a white majority on the commission.) Although Brown did not say so openly, it was clear from the tone of the e-mail that he considered this to be a "good thing" for Old Town.

The property developer promptly forwarded the e-mail to Representative Jones and Senator Black with the comment that they "might find this viewpoint interesting." Within 24 hours, the e-mail and angry responses to it from black political and community members were all over the front pages of the local newspaper. Many of the protestors were not only calling for Dave Brown's resignation from OTHA but also demanding that the Graves Manor purchase be taken off the table. Even though Brown's prospective developer had nothing to do with the Graves Manor property, the e-mail aroused fresh concerns about the motives of those who supported Graves Manor's sale to the medical school.

For most citizens, this was the first they had heard about the possible purchase of Graves Manor and the forced relocation of its residents. Although many members of the public supported any action that would keep the medical school in town, they were sympathetic and concerned for the fate of the Graves Manor residents. The residents themselves first heard about this solution by reading it in the paper, and they were outraged. A subsequent front-page article focused on their reactions. Barbara, a longtime resident, spoke for many when she said, "They're just ruining everybody's Christmas spirit."

The Decision Problem

City Administrator Thompson knew that support for the Graves Manor purchase could easily evaporate in the heat of the controversy. Any one, or all, of the parties involved could choose to back away from the purchase to avoid embarrassment.

Moreover, since he was in charge of the committee that came up with this solution and had persuaded the commission to go along with it, Thompson knew he might find himself used as a scapegoat if he could not find a way to calm the situation.

As he sat in his office, staring at the latest editorial on "the e-mail," he considered his options. Even though he agreed with the critics that Dave Brown should resign from the OTHA board, Thompson knew that the mayor, who had appointed Brown, would have to make that request. It would be awkward, with Brown being the local chair of the mayor's political party. Although the mayor campaigned on a nonpartisan platform of racial reconciliation, would he be willing to buck his political party chair?

Thompson also wondered what (if anything) he should do to reach out to black elected officials to reassure them that he had proposed the purchase of Graves Manor in good faith. What could he say or do to build trust?

Discussion Questions

1. Should City Administrator Ford Thompson have been proactive in making the public and the Graves Manor residents aware of the proposed purchase? If so, what could he or should he have done?
2. Should Thompson take the initiative and ask the mayor to pressure Brown to resign? If so, how should he approach that meeting?
3. Should Thompson take the initiative to reach out to black elected officials? If so, to whom should he reach out? What could or should he do to rebuild trust?
4. Should Thompson involve other actors in solving this problem? If so, who and how? In potentially volatile situations such as this one, what is the role of an administrator in dealing with policy boards and elected officials?

Suggested Simulation Roles

Ford Thompson, city administrator
John Rockefeller, mayor
Quincy Jones, state representative
James Black, state senator

If desired, expand the role-playing with these additions:
Medical school president
Developer
OTHA board member(s)
Members of the negotiating committee

Part V

Essential Management Practices

Introduction to Part V

Essential Management Practices

The Effective Local Government Manager addresses human resource, financial, and information technology management. Part V includes cases on the first two areas of management. Two of the three cases concern sticky personnel situations, while the third combines both a human resource and a budgetary issue.

The modern manager must be concerned with many aspects of effectiveness, including, for example, orchestrating solutions to problems presented for council consideration, reconciling differences in highly diverse communities, trying to get fair coverage from the local media, and evaluating organizational performance. However, that same manager also deals with traditional issues of recruiting, directing, developing, and even disciplining local employees.

The effective manager contributes in other ways. He or she helps identify revenue sources, finds ways to stretch the local budget, and ensures that the community maintains sound fiscal policy and practices. Even the smallest jurisdiction needs a set of personnel policies (leaves, holidays, hours of duty, for example) and a set of procedures for dealing with money (basic budget process, safeguarding cash, for example). The larger the jurisdiction, the thicker the policies and procedures manual is likely to be.

Case 12, "The Human Side of HR Decisions," illustrates what happens when a community acts before its policies are firmly in place. The city, to comply with a new state law, had to conduct background checks on all prospective employees. However, it continued to hire before the policies were actually in place to establish those checks and the procedures for following the new policies. As a result, the employment of a potentially excellent employee is jeopardized, and the city has to decide whether it can act in the absence of policy, even for good reason.

Similarities arise between Case 12 and Case 13, "Ethics and Internal Hiring": both involve decisions that must be made in the absence of supporting policy or procedure. In Case 13, a young manager's decision to promote internal hiring backfires when the only in-house candidate is not a good fit for the position. The manager must now choose: she can hire a person whose performance is dubious or go back on her promise to try to promote from within. Muddying the decision waters in this particular case is the history of favoritism frequently shown by the previous manager.

Case 14, "County Prison Overtime," originally appeared in *Managing Local Government: Cases in Decision Making* and is included here because of its emphasis on "making the numbers work." It illustrates that the budget is a process, not merely a document, and that budget decisions are made throughout the fiscal year as the adopted budget is implemented. In this particular case study, the issue is costly overtime in a vital county operation, the prison; however, the basic issue leads to acrimonious communication, challenges from one administrator to another—even concerns about the adequacy of law enforcement. The decision problem is complicated by the fact that there is no clear alternative and that the dispute then reaches the elected governing body. The case does not involve number crunching but illustrates very well what can happen in the course of a fiscal year.

The cases in Part V allow the reader to practice skills in several management practices, including staff effectiveness, diversity, policy facilitation, performance measurement, budgeting and financial analysis, human resource management, and integrity.

12

The Human Side of HR Decisions

Victoria Gordon

Background

Any employer has a responsibility to protect the public from harm caused by its employees. In today's employment environment, most job applicants expect that some form of reference checking or background investigation will occur before they are offered the position. In the public sector, there is often an even greater expectation by the public that public sector employees will have nothing in their history that might raise a red flag. For example, in a public school setting, where the safety of children is a primary concern, applicants for positions as administrators, teachers, aides, bus drivers, cafeteria workers, and even crossing guards get a thorough background check as a condition of employment—no exceptions.

For decades, municipalities in general have required background investigations for public safety positions—but not always for all positions in a municipality. In the past, this limited approach to background checks was customary, especially if the positions in question were not positions of trust—that is, if the employee had neither access to funds nor direct involvement in handling money. This limited approach was due in part to the cost of the background investigations and in part to whether there was any job-related reason for an intensive investigation.

In recent years, it has become commonplace to ask on employment applications whether the applicant has been convicted of a crime. Some applications specify that only the conviction of a felony need be reported, while still others add language that conviction of a crime will not necessarily preclude applicant's hiring. Some municipal employers allow a case-by-case consideration of the nature of the offense, frequency, and time lapsed since the last conviction. Obviously, applications for public safety positions would receive greater scrutiny from the municipality, and most municipalities hold those applicants to a higher standard than, say, an applicant for an administrative clerk position.

It is important for all employers, in consultation with their attorneys, to develop two things: (1) appropriate releases for reference checking and background investigations and (2) appropriate policies to respond to questionable results that are in compliance with applicable federal, state, and local laws.[1]

The Case

Bellflower is a midsize city in the Midwest with a population of 50,000. The city is considered the hub of economic development activity for the region, and it is located about an hour from the closest major metropolitan area. The city of Bellflower employs about 400 people.

On the morning of July 1, City Manager Cherrie Braeden received a memo from the human resource director, Jackson Smith, saying that because of action taken by the state legislature on the last day of the legislative session, the city is now required to conduct criminal background checks on all individuals hired, effective immediately. Smith stated that the HR department was working with the Municipal League to draft policies to address all components of this new law to make sure the city was in compliance. The proposed policies would go to the legal department, and then upon approval of the city attorney, Lloyd Phillips, HR would put the policies on the upcoming council agenda for consideration.

Among the changes proposed would be a provision adding the following language to all employment applications as well as to the city's Web pages, where position vacancies are listed: "For this type of employment, state law requires a state and national criminal history background check as a condition of employment."

In the meantime, the HR director suggested that only conditional offers of employment be made. HR would be contracting with a third-party administrator to provide on-demand employment background screening services on a temporary basis until the council adopted a formal policy to address the new legislation. Then the council would formally select a vendor to provide these services.

Smith asked for the city manager's approval on a memo he intended to e-mail to all city department heads that afternoon. The memo read as follows:

TO: All Department Heads
FROM: Jackson Smith, HR Director
DATE: July 1st
RE: Important Employment Information

At the end of the Legislative session, the State Legislature approved legislation pertaining to background investigations on all new hires for municipalities. The new law can be found on the legislative Web site. The primary purpose of this law is to ensure that anyone convicted of a sex offense will be barred from employment. However, the intent has resulted in actual language that affects the city and its hiring practices. The section of this new law that applies to municipalities reads that effective immediately the state "requires municipalities to ask all applicants to disclose their criminal history; requires municipalities to require a criminal record check; and establishes that conviction of a sex offense shall bar employment."

The City of Bellflower will be working toward developing policies that will bring our current hiring policies into compliance with the new law. The Department of Human Resources will facilitate all background checks pertaining to new hires. On a temporary basis, we will contract with Acme Security to conduct background checks. At this point, we are in the "catch up" mode in performing background checks on individuals who have been offered employment within the last few days. The background check process should be initiated after a candidate accepts a position. At this point, offers of employment should be conditional. It is recommended that candidates not begin work until after a background check has been completed.

Thank you in advance for your cooperation with this new hiring requirement. Should you have questions please feel free to contact me.

On July 2, Jackson Smith made a conditional offer of employment to Laura Andrews for an administrative assistant position in the clerk's office that involved occasional handling of cash and checks. Andrews had applied for the position at the beginning of June. She was in her late twenties and had five years administrative assistant experience. She was interviewed first by HR staff, and then came in for a second interview with the city clerk and HR director the following week.

Andrews conducted herself in a professional manner on each her visits to city hall, and everyone involved in the hiring process was in agreement that this candidate possessed the qualities they were looking for to fill this particular administrative assistant position. She accepted the conditional offer of employment and agreed to Smith's request for permission to conduct a background check, when he explained the need for it.

One week later, the HR director called the city manager to report there was a problem with Andrews's background check. Five years ago, she had been charged and convicted of theft by deception, for passing cold checks in an adjoining county in amounts that exceeded $300, which made the offense a class D felony. (A cold check is a check written for property or services that is not paid by the bank. A bank may dishonor a check for a number of reasons, but the most common reasons are that the account is closed, there is no account at all, or there are insufficient funds in the account to cover the check.)

Smith asked Cherrie Braeden how she wanted to proceed. He apologized for not having thought through the ramifications of implementing a new mandated policy from the state without any supporting city procedures, in the event there was a problem with a background check. Smith said, "I just didn't conceive of anyone agreeing to a background check if they knew they had a conviction. Really, I guess I knew it could happen, but I didn't think it would happen on the first person we ran a check on. I thought we would have some time to implement the appropriate personnel policies and think through the need for some kind of an appeal process to cope with extenuating circumstances."

The Decision Problem

Braeden was now faced with the uncomfortable task of having to instruct the HR director to withdraw the offer of employment, or identify alternatives. The new legislation did not cover what to do once the jurisdiction had the results of the background check, nor did it specifically prohibit hiring someone with a criminal conviction unless the conviction was for a sex crime. The new law merely said that the city must conduct the background investigation.

Braeden lists her alternatives:

1. Instruct Smith to withdraw the offer with no explanation to Andrews.
2. Talk to HR, talk to the legal department, and then make a decision.
3. Talk to HR, legal, and Andrews, and then make a decision.
4. Involve the council in the decision.

The city manager soon realized that she faced a complex problem. The city had not considered what would constitute an acceptable or compelling reason to discount the findings of a background check, or whether it would allow an applicant an appeal to contest the findings of the background check. It seemed to Braeden that, at a minimum, when staff developed a new policy, consideration would be given to the specific duties of the position, the number of offenses and circumstances of each offense, the recentness of the conviction, whether the conviction arose out of an employment situation, the circumstances of the conviction, and the accuracy of the explanation provided by the applicant regarding the nature of the conviction. But in the meantime, without a formal city policy in place, how should the city address the dilemma of complying with a new state law while at the same time treating a potential new employee fairly?

There was something else nagging at Cherrie Braeden's conscience. She recalled an incident twenty-eight years ago in her own past that involved a financial near disaster and a bad check. Had she not straightened the whole thing out with the bank, and convinced them to reverse the bank service charges, she, too, might have been charged with an offense similar to Andrews's.

Was there some extenuating circumstance that might explain what happened? If so, could she give Andrews the benefit of the doubt? Or was her own past experience coloring her judgment of the Andrews situation? The administrative assistant position in question would not be hard to fill. But what was the city's moral obligation to an applicant who had originally applied and interviewed without notification that a background check would eventually be required?

With fifteen years' experience as a city manager, Cherrie Braeden had long since earned a reputation as a fair and decisive decision maker. However, she decided to wait until the next day to further explore her options with her staff. In the meantime, even with her experience, she was comfortable calling one or two people for advice. She picked up the phone and dialed two trusted colleagues in neighboring cities, who would, of course, also be adopting policies to comply with the new state legislation. They helped her to weigh the pros and cons of all her alternatives and decide what to do.

The next morning Braeden went to consult the HR director and the city attorney. Lloyd Phillips, the city attorney, offered to call the prosecuting attorney in the neighboring county to see what he could find out informally about the case. On advice from the attorney later that same morning, the city manager decided to speak to Andrews personally about what had happened in her past. Without elaborating, Jackson Smith invited Laura Andrews back to city hall for a meeting that afternoon with the city manager.

Andrews readily agreed to meet. Cherrie Braeden explained that they thought she would be an asset to the city workforce. However, the city had an obligation to protect the interests of the citizens and thus must take seriously her conviction for theft by deception. When the city manager explained that they were under advice from counsel to rescind her offer of employment if she could not provide a satisfactory reason for her conviction. In response, Andrews pulled a file from her briefcase.

Andrews admitted that she was taken off guard by Jackson Smith's request that she agree to the background check when she last met with him, and she regretted not taking the opportunity to express her concerns. She apologized that her questionable history came as a surprise to the HR director. She said, "I never meant to deceive you in any way. I was just too embarrassed to say anything, and then when I got home I thought of calling you, but I just didn't know whether I would be making things worse. I really need this job, and I didn't want to jeopardize my chances."

As the conversation progressed, Andrews explained the cold check incident. From the papers she had brought to this meeting, she was able to provide legal documentation that proved the conviction was a one-time occurrence related to the division of assets during her nasty divorce. Her husband closed the bank account in question without telling her, and she continued to write checks on the account. Because her then-husband had gone against a court order when he closed the bank account, he was ordered by the judge to reimburse Laura Andrews for all the financial costs associated with the incident. However, there was nothing she could do to make the felony on her record go away. On advice of her divorce attorney, she had not fought the charges because she did not have the money for an adequate legal defense.

During the past five years prior to her offer from the city of Bellflower, Andrews had worked for a small company that was owned by friends of her family. However, they had recently sold the business when they decided to retire. She explained that she had known for quite some time that she would be losing her job but had not anticipated that it would take so long to find a new one. At the end of their meeting, the city manager asked Andrews to leave copies of the supporting documentation from her file, thanked her for meeting with them, and told her that they would contact her the next day with their final decision.

Discussion Questions

1. If you were City Manager Cherrie Braeden, whom would you have called for advice in this situation? If she had called you, what advice would you have given her?
2. What does Braeden really owe Laura Andrews, the applicant? Is she letting her experiences color her decision? Should Braeden have called the applicant and offered her a chance to explain?
3. What are the competing values for the city manager? Are there ethical considerations in this case that need to be identified? How might the ICMA Code of Ethics with Guidelines assist the city manager in making a decision?
4. If we further learned that Andrews had excellent employment references, would that knowledge have changed your decision on how to advise the city manager to proceed? Conversely, what if she had poor references or just adequate references? How would that evaluative information have affected your decision? What if the position she was applying for was a department head position—how would that have affected your decision?
5. What do you agree with in terms of how this case was handled up to this point?
6. What do you disagree with in terms of how this case was handled up to this point?
7. Assuming the city manager turns to the city attorney, Lloyd Phillips, for advice, does that mean his advice should be followed in the making of the final hiring decision?
8. Identify obstacles and opportunities that might help you to decide how to resolve this problem.
9. In general, what can we learn from the experiences of those involved in this case?

Suggested Simulation Roles

Cherrie Braeden, city manager
Jackson Smith, human resource director
Lloyd Phillips, city attorney
Laura Andrews, job applicant

Note

1 For more complete discussion of this topic, see William J. Woska, "Legal Issues for HR Professionals: Reference Checking/Background Investigations," *Public Personnel Management* 36 (Spring 2007): 79–89.

13

Ethics and Internal Hiring

Tim Styka, April Konitzer, Michael Richards, Derek Jablonicky, and Lea Kitz

Background

In northern Wisconsin, just a few miles off Highway 51, the land opens up to rolling hills filled with a mix of old hardwood and newer pine and birch forests. The population density along the red dirt and iron-stained roads of this area is sparse, but small and medium-sized communities dot the map.

The city of Pioneer Falls is not only the county seat but also the central community for shopping, worship, and limited health care. It once was a thriving logging town: from here logs floated downstream on the Wisconsin River to the mills. However, logging has largely disappeared, just as the prior economic base—trapping—had disappeared. Now the main source of revenue for the residents and the local units of government comes from a few small manufacturing facilities and seasonal, tourism-based activities.

The last census confirmed that the city of Pioneer Falls had grown from 2,916 to 4,212 residents (about one-third) as a result of tourism jobs in the area and an unexpectedly high number of births. Emigration from Illinois and other surrounding states added to the population as these newcomers sought the simpler life of Pioneer Falls.

Growth has not been without its costs, however. The community has seen an increase in nuisance crimes such as vandalism and petty theft, mostly involving vehicles. In addition, residents' use of marijuana and methamphetamines is increasing at rates approximating the state average: nearly 20 percent for marijuana use, and 6 percent for methamphetamines. City officials have been working on a comprehensive plan to deal with this illegal behavior. For now, law enforcement for Pioneer Falls is provided through a contract with the sheriff's department, and the city also contracts for 80 hours a month of patrol time in the community.

The higher tax base, resulting from increased growth, has meant an influx of funds to address some emerging issues. The city liked the idea of giving the youth in the community more recreational programs and park improvements. Traditionally, parks and recreation efforts were limited to youth basketball, baseball, and softball sponsored by nonprofit organizations such as the Falls Soccer Club, Pioneer Bulldog Football, and Falls Hoops. The initial push for a formalized parks and recreation program came from a group of parents. For example, parents in Pioneer Falls and adjoining communities organized an informal hockey program. But citizens were beginning to think that the city itself should be doing more to provide parks and recreation services.

The lack of adequate parks and youth recreational activities also bothered Maxwell Ott, the city administrator, who thought it reflected poorly on him. His cause gained momentum when a wealthy landowner provided a significant bequest for city programs. With private seed money in hand and increasing tax revenues to sustain the program, the city budgeted for a new parks and recreation department and began to create a framework for its governance and mission.

Ott then set out to hire the first director for the department. However, the employee pool was a shallow one. The city interviewing committee came up with three potential candidates to consider for the position, and Ott pushed to hire one of them, Chad Anderson, as parks and recreation manager.

Anderson had served the community for over twenty-five years as the high school physical education teacher and was on the same bowling team as Maxwell Ott. He had considerable experience in recreational activities; however, his managerial abilities in budgeting and personnel were limited. Nevertheless, with the strong backing of the city administrator, Chad Anderson was offered the position with the city and was approved by the city council.

Internally, the hire was not popular. Ott had not developed a positive work environment during his term as city administrator. City employees were seldom offered internal promotions. There was little training and team building. Employees did not receive annual performance reviews or an opportunity to develop individualized work plans with the administrator or their superiors. There were cries of cronyism and an us-versus-them atmosphere in city offices. The Anderson hire, which occurred without a formal job description or job requirements, was only the latest example of the way Ott handled personnel matters.

Shortly after Anderson's hiring, the city council, sensitive to continuing high turnover and frequent employee complaints, undertook a performance review of the administration. Maxwell Ott voluntarily retired rather than risking being fired.

The city council interviewed a host of candidates for the position of city administrator, ultimately focusing on Susan Hanson as the front-runner. The council was impressed with her fresh ideas and professional qualifications. Hanson brought with her processes and procedures that addressed all of the concerns held by the council—chiefly, personnel management, budgeting, and capital management. Her credentials included a master's degree in public administration and fifteen years' experience as a city administrator in a town of 9,000 in a far northern suburb of Chicago. Like many other suburbanites, she was looking for a lower key place like Pioneer Falls to settle down.

Her employment with Pioneer Falls was sealed when she presented her list of key tactics the city could incorporate in its hiring and promotional practices. Hanson was generally aware of the city's high level of employee dissatisfaction, so she came prepared, offering the hiring team alternative methods for managing the city's human resources.

Susan Hanson appeared to be the ideal candidate to meet the challenges of Pioneer Falls. However, it was these same credentials and initiatives that would come back to haunt her. During the questioning part of the interview process, a council woman asked her how she would go about gaining the trust of the employees and building a more cohesive governmental work unit. Hanson described a hiring plan for the city that would include an internal hiring protocol, with the benefit of bolstering the dampened morale of city employees.

Specifically, to raise the level of morale within the small city administration, Susan Hanson proposed not only to emphasize internal hiring but also to set up a plan for career planning and training and development. During the interview she told the interview team, "We need to let our hardworking employees know that I am going to do whatever I can to help them realize the position they want within the city, as long as they continue to work hard and strive to do jobs they may not feel comfortable with right away."

When the interview team asked her about prior experiences she stated, "I am a firm believer in on-the-job training. Even though I am an outsider to this community, I am aware of the legal and moral ramifications of improper selection and promotional processes. I have no doubt that my education and work ethic will allow me to build coalitions and get the job done right for the taxpayers of Pioneer Falls."

Susan Hanson was able to answer all the questions to the satisfaction of the interview team. She soon received and accepted an offer letter, and her appointment was quickly approved by the full city council. The council wanted to put the failings of the previous administrator behind it, and thus it quickly embraced the new and innovative ideas of the young professional who portrayed immense energy and appreciation for the job.

The Case

Within a few months after Susan Hanson settled into her cramped office in the Pioneer Falls city hall, Parks and Recreation Manager Chad Anderson popped into her office to inform her of his intention to retire. He wanted her to know that even though he was friends with Maxwell Ott, his intent to retire had nothing to do with her appointment. As he stated, "My youngest just had twins, and I now have eight grandchildren total. At 68, I don't know how much time I will have to enjoy retirement, but I suppose it is time to go sooner or later. Good luck."

With Anderson's resignation in hand, Susan Hanson had a chance to test her new hiring policy. She worked with members of a city council subcommittee to refine the policy, and a majority of the city council then voted to approve it. Armed with the policy, she began to look for a new parks and recreation manager.

The hiring policy stipulated a number of conditions for filling a position within the city with internal and external candidates. As predicted, the policy stated a preference for promoting from within the organization. Susan Hanson had interviewed leaders of other cities, and the majority of them believed that the happiest employees were those who had opportunities for professional and personal growth.

This confirmed the wisdom of her original plan to advertise the parks and recreation manager position internally before announcing it externally. Having been on board with the city for several months now, she had come to know a number of her employees rather well. She would even go so far as to say that she probably could have determined—from considering the entire group of fifty part-time, temporary, and full-time employees—which one would make the best candidate to lead the parks and recreation department.

Chad Anderson's retirement from parks and recreation needed to be filled quickly. However, because her predecessor had done such a poor job of maintaining human resource information, Hanson had no job description to adapt. Moreover, the compact city administration lacked an HR professional on staff whom Hanson could ask to analyze the job and help develop an updated job description. So, with limited information gained from brief conversations with the retiring manager in the closing weeks before his departure, she set out to craft a job description for the open slot.

Determining a candidate's ideal level of education was Hanson's first obstacle. In her previous city, finding qualified candidates with advanced degrees was not an issue. Here, however, she predicted it would be harder to find highly educated, experienced managers with ideal skill sets. In fact, at present, she was the only city employee with an advanced degree. Thus Pioneer Falls traditionally contracted with an outside lawyer to serve as city attorney and used external engineering firms on a project basis.

Hanson finally decided she needed an outside opinion on the education level for the department manager position. On the advice of the human resource director at her former city, she decided to keep the education level vague. The resulting job description required the applicant to have a minimum of a high school diploma, with a bachelor's degree preferred. Further, the description stated a preference for applicants with experience in budgeting as well as some management experience.

Hanson submitted the job description to the council committee charged with personnel, where it was approved. In accordance with her new hiring policy, the job description was circulated to all employees through a combination of e-mails and postings on the job boards at the various city locations where employees congregated for breaks.

Employees were allowed ten working days to apply for the open position. If there were no candidates, the job would be posted externally, in the city newspaper and regional dailies. If she did not find suitable applicants after two weeks, she planned to expand her search to the two largest state daily newspapers in an effort to expand the hiring pool. She was not allowing lengthy intervals between stages in the hiring process because the longer the position remained unfilled, the more work it was imposing on other city employees.

In the meantime, city employees were talking about the open parks and recreation manager position—mainly in terms of the qualifications. The description on the job board included budget experience as well as some knowledge of personnel techniques, such as scheduling and hiring, which affect a number of limited-term and seasonal jobs within the parks department. What the job description didn't articulate—but employees generally knew was necessary—was the need for a manager who could really deliver visible services to the public. In addition, the person hired would be actively soliciting funds from the public as well as networking to get donations for equipment and volunteers for some program activities.

One internal candidate, Paul Garrett, wanted the position very badly. Having been with the city in public works for a number of years, he thought that his years of service were deserving of a promotion and a raise with the city. Garrett had minimal management skills and had performed poorly as a city employee, but because of the former administrator's lax personnel practices, including inattention to performance evaluations, there was nothing in Garrett's file documenting his weaknesses. Garrett submitted an application for manager of the parks and recreation department.

When the ten business days for internal candidates to apply elapsed, Hanson found to her surprise that she had only one internal candidate: Paul Garrett. She now had a conundrum: there *was* no pool from which to consider the best applicant, and the policy did not address the possibility of only one internal employee applying for a job. In addition, while she was aware of Garrett's poor performance, she did not have the written documentation of it to justify denying his application.

Garrett was known in the city and by the council. He had attended one year at the local community college before starting to work for the city of Pioneer Falls collecting waste and recyclables. As created, the job description was broad enough to allow an applicant like Garrett, who met the education minimum of a high school diploma and had enough work experience with the city, to make a case for his hiring.

To his credit, Garrett had taken the time to understand the new internal hiring process and expected to use it to his advantage with future city job openings. Moreover, after conversations with staff at the city, he was fairly sure he was going to be the only internal candidate to apply for the position.

Susan Hanson's instincts and her experience told her that Garrett was not the right candidate for the position. For one thing, this position was crucial in the city's fight against drugs. She worried that promoting Paul Garrett to parks and recreation director would violate the ICMA Code of Ethics.

But she also knew that if she did not follow the internal hiring policy she had worked so hard to create and see adopted by the city council, she might appear to be going against everything she promised during her own interview to become city administrator. If Paul Garrett were denied the job based purely on hearsay, the city might even face a legal suit. In her mind the problem did not stop there. She was concerned that a deviation from her policy, even if the candidate had questionable abilities and character, could cause her employees to lose their faith and trust in her.

Never before in her fifteen years of experience had she faced such an issue. She blamed herself: not only did she write the job description but she also created a policy that she now doubted would meet the needs of the city and internal staff. Going forward, this might not be the only job opening for which there would be no suitable internal candidate.

Sitting in her office, she mentally reviewed various scenarios to remedy this situation. The deadline for action on the application, in accordance with the new hiring policy, was less than twenty-four hours away. She needed to arrive at an answer—the right answer.

Discussion Questions

1. What are the ramifications that City Administrator Susan Hanson should consider before deciding not to hire Paul Garrett as parks and recreation manager? What ethical dilemmas confront her?
2. How can the city administrator maintain a high level of employee morale when it is not appropriate to hire an eager internal candidate?
3. How could the new city administrator have addressed personnel issues originating in a previous administration?
4. What preventive steps could have been put in place prior to writing the job description, to reduce the city administrator's exposure to liability in the hiring process?
5. Could the job description have been written differently to anticipate this situation of having only one internal applicant? How about the hiring policy?
6. Would a job analysis have been useful before the job description was written? If so, why? If not, why not?

Suggested Simulation Roles

Susan Hanson, city manager
City council members
City department heads

14

County Prison Overtime

Tom Mills

Background

Franklin County is a suburban-rural county located in one of the Mid-Atlantic states. It adjoins a large eastern city and has a land area of 650 square miles; a population of approximately 500,000; and forty-five local governments that consist of boroughs, villages, and townships. The local governments have their own police forces but lack secure holding facilities for defendants who have been arrested and bound over by local magistrates for trial in the county courts.

The county provides all its criminal justice system services from the county courthouse located in Franklinville, the county seat. On a tract of county-owned land just outside of Franklinville, the county operates two detention facilities: a small, medium-security facility for juveniles and a large, modern, medium-security facility for both male and female adult detainees. The latter facility, called the county prison, has a capacity of approximately 340 inmates and is maintained and operated by a staff of 181 employees.

Franklin County's chief lawmaking and administrative authority is the elected county commission, which is vested with both executive and legislative powers. Voters also elect a number of administrative officers—including the sheriff, the controller, and the district attorney—and the judges of the county court, which is called the supreme court of common pleas.

The county commission consists of three members elected countywide for four-year terms. The county code requires that one of the three commissioners be a member of the opposing, or minority, party. The county is predominantly Republican, and members of that party regularly control the countywide elective offices. The county commission, perhaps owing to its higher visibility, has occasionally been controlled by a Democratic majority.

The county commissioners appoint a county administrator, all nonelected department heads, and the members of most county boards and commissions. The day-to-day operation of the county is the responsibility of the county administrator—a professional local government manager who is recruited and appointed on the basis of technical competence. The county boasts a commitment to professionalism. The county administrator recruits and hires his or her own staff and has been responsible for securing the appointments of the finance director, the personnel director, and the director of purchasing.

The county code constrains the county commissioners' powers of appointment in some instances. The power to appoint the director of the department of corrections, who oversees both the county prison and the juvenile rehabilitation center, is vested in a prison board. The prison board is composed of the president judge of the supreme court of common pleas (or that judge's designee), the district attorney, the sheriff, the controller, and the three county commissioners. Five of the seven members of the board were Republicans at the time this case begins.

The Case

In the previous election, the Democratic party had won the majority of seats on the county commission by taking what proved to be the more popular position on a critical environmental issue. In hopes of reelection, the Democratic commissioners instituted a cost-containment program that, if successful, would enable them to complete their term without raising taxes. The commissioners issued a directive to all department heads instructing them to implement economies wherever possible. The county administrator, George Truly, was given the principal responsibility for implementing the cost-containment program. He, in turn, had charged the finance director, Donald Dexter, with much of the program's operating responsibility.

After monitoring the expenditures of the county prison, Dexter was convinced that overtime expenditures were out of control. He had met on several occasions with Charles Goodheart, the director of corrections, and had called him almost weekly in an effort to reduce overtime costs. In Dexter's view, those contacts had been of little value, since overtime expenditures continued at what he regarded as an excessive rate. Somewhat reluctantly, he decided to go on record. He dictated what was to be the first in a series of memorandums sent electronically.

March 12
TO: Charles R. Goodheart, Director of Corrections
FROM: Donald D. Dexter, Finance Director
SUBJECT: Excessive Prison Overtime

Pursuant to the county commissioners' directive of January 8 establishing the cost containment program, my staff and I have been closely monitoring the overtime expenditures incurred in the operation of the county prison. We have had several meetings and numerous telephone conversations regarding this matter with both you and your key staff members—all to no avail. Overtime expenditures have continued to rise and might well exceed the budget allocation. This I find to be particularly distressing, since we had every hope that this was one area of your operation in which we could effect significant savings.

I would greatly appreciate it if you would provide me, at your first opportunity, with a detailed justification for the current rate of overtime usage and your plans to keep such expenditures to an absolute minimum.

cc: George S. Truly, County Administrator
Frank Friendly, Personnel Director

Before sending this memorandum, Dexter had given considerable thought to its wording and had concluded that, even if the memorandum was a bit strong, it was warranted in this situation.

In the weeks that followed, Dexter continued to scrutinize the prison payroll records but did not observe any reduction in the use of overtime. He was about to schedule yet another meeting with Goodheart when he received the following memorandum through the interoffice mail.

April 5
TO: Donald D. Dexter, Finance Director
FROM: Charles R. Goodheart, Director of Corrections
SUBJECT: Response to Your Request for Information Regarding Overtime Expenditures

You indicated in your e-mail of March 12 that you thought we were utilizing an excessive amount of overtime. I welcome the opportunity to explain what might appear to be excessive overtime usage, but which really is no more than prudent prison management.

You will recall that during the budget hearings last year, I shared with you information on overtime usage in the four surrounding counties. Each of these counties has a comparable prison system, and, as I noted then, each uses more overtime than we do.

You must remember that I requested $434,400 as an overtime allocation for the current fiscal year (including holiday overtime). The overtime figure that was allocated to this department was substantially less. When budget allocations were announced, there was no explanation for the reduced overtime figure other than a general statement—which certainly is appropriate for you as finance director to make—that times were difficult, money was tight, and every effort must be made to curtail unnecessary expenditures.

Although I accept these comments in the spirit in which they were made, I still am held responsible and accountable to the prison board for operating a safe and secure correctional institution. Prisons are potentially very dangerous, and that danger can be averted only by keeping staffing levels at safe and realistic levels.

As we both know, there are many justifiable causes for overtime usage in a prison setting. In the following paragraphs I'll attempt to identify the major causes.

Turnover. During last year and continuing into this year, we have experienced high levels of turnover among our correctional officers. When staff members leave, we are required to fill their posts, which we do through the use of overtime. The problem continues during recruitment for replacements and during the three-week training course to which all recruits are sent. When you add the two- to four-week delay in filling positions to the three-week training period, you can readily see that a considerable amount of overtime might be involved.

Turnover is perhaps our most critical problem. Previously I sent you a detailed commentary on our turnover experience. Over the past several years, I have told everyone willing to listen that there is a strong relationship between turnover in a correctional institution and overtime expenditures.

First of all, entry-level correctional officers are poorly paid and, as I've told the county commissioners at every budget hearing, that is certainly true in our case. Second, this is a very difficult profession. Prison personnel are continually required to work at very high stress levels. Finally, we enjoy very little public esteem, and the working conditions can on occasion be very unpleasant. It's a small wonder that there is high turnover not only in our prisons but in prisons all across this country. When a staff member leaves, the need to fill the post continues. Unless the prison board tells me that it does not want me to fill vacant posts, I will continue to do so, and I have no choice but to use overtime.

Hospital watches. Whenever an inmate requires inpatient treatment in a local hospital, I must provide the necessary security. Recently, two inmates were hospitalized. For each day of hospitalization, we provided two correctional officers per shift, three shifts per day, for a total of

(continued)

forty-eight hours of coverage. As you can see, the time mounts up rapidly. We have no fat in our shift complements; therefore, when a need like this arises, it must be covered with overtime.

Emergency situations. Whenever there is reason to believe that inmates might be planning an action that could endanger the security of the institution, I adopt an emergency plan that puts all supervisors on twelve-hour shifts. I do not place this institution on an emergency footing for any trivial or illusory cause. Those instances in which I have used emergency overtime have been fully justified, and I stand by my actions.

Sick leave. Our sick leave usage compares favorably with that of other county departments that enjoy less trying working conditions. Still, when a correctional officer calls in sick, his or her position must be filled, and it is usually filled by the use of overtime. We can't call in a replacement on one hour's notice on the person's day off, upset his or her family life, and worsen a bad morale situation simply to cover an eight-hour shift. We think that the use of overtime in these situations is the most sensible solution.

Workers' compensation. I have frequently remarked on this problem in the past. Today we are filling two posts that are vacant as a result of workers' compensation claims against the county. When an employee is injured on the job and a doctor certifies that he or she may not work, I have no choice but to utilize overtime to fill the post. I simply don't have any slack resources that would permit me to do otherwise.

Reserve duty. Under the laws of this state, all staff members who are members of bona fide military reserve units are authorized to take fifteen days of paid military leave annually. When they depart for their military training, their posts remain, and we are responsible for filling them. The problem is exacerbated by the tendency of both military leave and vacations to cluster in the summer months. Another aspect of military reserve duty also generates overtime. Our correctional officers are scheduled around the clock and frequently are scheduled to work on a weekend when they are expected to attend reserve drills. Under the policy adopted by the county commissioners, the reservists may take "no-pay" time and fulfill their reserve obligations, while the county saves their straight-time pay. I am forced to use overtime to fill their posts.

Vacations. We do make a concerted effort to schedule vacations so as not to result in overtime expenditures. Unfortunately, as a direct result of our lean staffing, on occasion we must resort to overtime to permit our correctional officers to enjoy the vacations they have earned.

Training programs. Compared to the standard advocated by national authorities, our training efforts are extremely modest. We provide equal employment opportunity training, particularly with respect to our female correctional officers, and some supervisory training. In addition, we provide training in interpersonal communication skills—training I regard as essential in an institution such as ours. Since our shift schedules contain no fat, personnel must be brought in for training on their days off, which, of course, results in overtime.

The major causes of our overtime expenditures are as noted above. I have brought these problems and their causes to the attention of the county commissioners at every budget hearing over the past nine years. Our staff utilization records and overtime documentation are available to anyone who wishes to review them. We have nothing to hide.

I don't mean to be flippant or discourteous but frankly, I'm no wizard. I cannot operate this institution without a reasonable overtime allocation any more than the Jews of antiquity could make bricks without straw. For you to insist that I do so strikes me as being every bit as unreasonable as was the order of the Pharaoh's overseer.

(continued)

> If you can provide specific suggestions regarding policies or methodologies that you feel will assist in overtime reduction without compromising safe and efficient operation of this institution, please be assured that we will be happy to work with you in implementing them. We are open to any thoughtful and constructive recommendations that you or your staff may have. In the meantime, you might consider funding a comprehensive study of our staffing needs, including the need for overtime, by a nationally recognized group specializing in the field of corrections.
>
> cc: Members of the County Prison Board
> George S. Truly, County Administrator
> Frank Friendly, Personnel Director

Dexter read the memorandum twice, his feelings alternating between anger and frustration. He regarded Goodheart highly, knowing him to be a caring individual and a respected corrections professional. "But clearly," thought Dexter, "he's no administrator. I asked him for a detailed justification of his use of overtime and his plans to keep those expenditures to a minimum, and what did he do? He offered me a lesson in biblical history and tried to put the monkey on my back with that bit about 'any thoughtful and constructive recommendations' I might have—baloney!"

Dexter further noted that Goodheart had twice mentioned his accountability to the county prison board and had been ungracious enough to copy the prison board members on the memorandum. "That," thought Dexter sourly, "is just a brazen example of saber rattling. Maybe he thinks that he can get me off his case if he can broaden the controversy by bringing in the prison board. Not likely!" Still angry, he spun in his chair, picked up his headset and microphone, and started to use the voice recognition software on his computer.

Meanwhile, Jim Kirby, chair of the county commission, was enjoying his new role. He was no stranger to county government: he had been the minority commissioner for eight years under Republican administrations, but that, he felt, was essentially a naysayer role. Now, as the chair during a Democratic administration, he was in a position to take the lead on policy decisions, and he was enjoying it. He had founded a successful business in the county and had called the shots there for more than thirty years. Although Kirby had often mused that government and business were much more different than alike—at least on paper—he relished his leadership role in the county.

Kirby prided himself on his capacity for work and made every effort to keep on top of things. He regretted that he had not read Corrections Director Goodheart's memorandum of April 5 before attending the monthly prison board meeting. He hated to be blindsided. The presiding judge of the supreme court of common pleas, Harvey Strickland, who was also president of the prison board, had shown Kirby his printout of the Goodheart memorandum as well as a copy of Dexter's memorandum of March 12, which had prompted Goodheart's reply.

Strickland had been his usual amiable self, but Kirby knew from long experience that with Strickland you worried not about what he said but about what he left unsaid. The fact that Strickland had brought the memorandums with him to the meeting and his oblique references to "those in this life who are penny-wise and pound-foolish" convinced Kirby that trouble was brewing.

As soon as Kirby got back to his office, he called George Truly, the county administrator, and asked him to stop by. Truly was the perfect balance to Kirby. Kirby was born to lead—an activist by nature—full of ideas and restless energy and impatient with detail. Truly, on the other hand, was a doer. A professional administrator with substantial background in local government, he disliked the publicity and pressure of policy leadership, preferring instead the satisfaction that came from making policies work and seeing that services were delivered. The two men understood each other and had developed an effective working relationship. Neither one worried about the line between policy and administration. Each one understood the overlap between the two activities and freely advised the other about county problems.

As Truly walked through the doorway, Kirby asked him, "Are you familiar with Don Dexter's memo of March 12 and Charlie Goodheart's reply?"

Truly said that he was and that he had already spoken to Dexter about them, but that he had been too late.

"What do you mean 'too late'?" Kirby asked. "This thing looks to me like it can still be salvaged."

"Then," Truly replied, "I guess you haven't seen Don's memorandum of April 7."

April 7
TO: Charles R. Goodheart, Director of Corrections
FROM: Donald D. Dexter, Finance Director
SUBJECT: Your Evasive Memorandum of April 5

In a sincere effort to implement the county commissioners' directive establishing a countywide cost containment program, I wrote to you on March 12. In my e-memorandum I asked you to provide me with a detailed justification for the current rate of overtime usage and your plans to keep such expenditures to an absolute minimum.

In reply, you gave me three pages of generalities and gratuitous comments. You're the prison expert, not me. If I had any good ideas on how you could run your operation more efficiently or economically, you can be sure I'd offer them. But as I see it, that's your job, not mine. My job is to see to the financial well-being of this county, and I can't do my job if I don't get cooperation.

That's all I'm asking for—your cooperation in achieving the goals set for all of us by the county commissioners. Your knowledge of the Old Testament is better than mine, but I do know that the Pharaoh didn't pay overtime. As far as I am concerned, you can have all the straw you want, but cut down on the overtime.

The Decision Problem

After Commission Chair Kirby had finished reading Dexter's memo of April 7, he sighed wearily, laid it aside, looked up at Truly, and said, "I see what you mean. Any suggestions?"

Truly was a career administrator who had spent twenty-two years in a series of increasingly demanding city management jobs before being recruited by Kirby to serve as Franklin County administrator. He had been given full authority in the recruitment of his administrative staff, and he had picked, among others, Don Dexter. Not only was Dexter extremely bright but he also had been the controller for a large manufacturing firm in the county—quite an accomplishment for a man who was not yet thirty. "But," Truly reflected, "he's never swum in political waters before, and there's no question that he's in over his head."

As the two men reviewed the situation, they tried to define the problem specifically, to identify possible courses of action, and to anticipate the probable outcomes of those alternatives.

It was evident that whatever they did, they had to do it quickly. Strickland could not yet have seen Dexter's memorandum of April 7. If he had, he would have had it with him at the meeting, and he would not have been so affable.

The cost-containment program was important to Kirby and the other Democrat on the county commission. It was probably their best hope for reelection. If they exempted the county prison from the program for fear of what the prison board might do, the program could be weakened throughout the county. After all, why should the other departments conform if the prison wasn't expected to do its part?

Under the county code, the prison board, not the county commission, was responsible for approving all prison-related expenditures. With its Republican majority, the board could give Goodheart a blank check if they wanted to and the commissioners would be able to do nothing about it. "Well not exactly nothing," groused Kirby. "We could direct the county solicitor to sue the prison board, but since the president of the board is also the president judge, that's more of a theoretical than a practical remedy."

In fact, it was much more likely that the prison board would wind up suing the county commissioners. If the board alleged that an imminent threat to public safety was created by the refusal of the commissioners and their agents to fund the county prison adequately, it could bring an action *in mandamus*. In that event, the prison board would not be likely to limit the action to the question of prison overtime but would, in all likelihood, open a Pandora's box of problems. Goodheart had documented many of these problems in his memorandum of April 5, and that memo would probably be Exhibit A at a trial. Issues most likely to be litigated included the needs for adequate prison staffing levels, proactive strategies to combat the high rate of turnover, and higher salaries for correctional officers.

Kirby knew that if political warfare broke out, the Republicans would move quickly to seize the high ground. They would allege that the Democrats were jeopardizing the safety and tranquility of the community for the sake of a few paltry dollars. Kirby was too old a hand to suppose that arguments of efficiency and economy would carry any weight with the public in such a debate—especially if citizens were convinced that they were going to be murdered in their beds.

Since all the elected officials in the county were Republicans with the exception of Kirby and the other Democratic commissioner, they could really make things untenable. So far, the elected officials had been cooperating in the cost-containment program. If, however, they chose to support the prison board in a confrontation with the commission, the cost-containment program would be thoroughly scuttled.

"Don Dexter really put us in a box," remarked Kirby.

"Yes, but he's young and bright. He won't make the same mistake again," replied Truly.

"If the president judge gets him in his sights, he won't have the opportunity," observed Kirby solemnly.

"Funny thing," Kirby continued. "Don was right—that memorandum from Charlie was evasive, but Don should have known better than to say so. More than that, he shouldn't have written at all, much less send an e-mail to a guy like Charlie. In a situation like that, you go to see the guy. E-mail is a very incomplete, very limited way to communicate. It's a lot easier to talk tough to your computer than to an adversary. My rules have always been to never write a letter if you can avoid it, and never throw one away."

After almost an hour of discussion, the two men had identified five alternative approaches to the problem. Unfortunately, none of them was without risk.

1. Exempt the prison from the cost-containment program. Under this alternative, Kirby would contact Strickland informally and intimate that the commission would not be unduly concerned if the prison did not achieve its cost containment objectives. The justification offered would be that, as a public safety and law enforcement agency, the prison ought not be held to the same standard of cost reduction as other agencies, lest public safety suffer. The main problem with this approach was that party loyalty was paramount in this county, and Strickland was certain to share this information with the other elected officials—especially the district attorney and the sheriff, who headed justice system agencies. Once the commissioners had yielded on the prison, it would be difficult for them to hold the line on other justice system agencies, and the cost-containment program would be seriously jeopardized. The result could be that the majority commissioners would be branded as weak men of little resolve. And that could have serious spillover effects in other areas.
2. Fund an in-depth study of the prison by a nationally recognized group specializing in corrections. Since this was a solution proposed by the director of corrections, it would most likely gain the acceptance of the prison board. Apart from the cost of such a study, which could be considerable, its recommendations were not likely to be favorable to the county administration. Through long experience, Kirby and Truly had come to believe that special-interest groups of any ilk rarely supported anything antithetical to their special interest. Worse yet, a comprehensive study might only document and verify the types of complaints that the director of corrections had been making for years. It was one thing to ignore his complaints; it would be something quite different were the county administration to ignore the studied recommendations of nationally recognized experts.
3. Conduct an in-house study of the need for prison overtime. This alternative had a good deal to recommend it. The county had a small management analysis team that reported directly to the county administrator. The supervisor of the team was a thoroughly honest and objective career professional who had been a founding member of the Association of Management Analysts in State and Local Government and was well respected both within the county and beyond its borders. The problem, of course, was one of credibility. Despite his excellent reputation, his objectivity might be questioned in the partisan political climate that prevailed in Franklin County. Moreover, the prison board might refuse to approve such a study. A study could be undertaken without the prison board's concurrence, as a prerogative of the majority commissioners, but in that event, the prison board might view the study as flawed.
4. Attempt to find an honest broker to conduct a study of prison overtime. "Honest" in this context meant someone who would be considered honest in the eyes of the prison board—someone they would perceive as having no ax to grind. Ideally, this person should already work for the county and be known by, and enjoy the confidence of, the prison board. The downside of this alternative, assuming that such a person could be found, was that the honest broker might not be all that honest. Should such a person be selected with the prison board's concurrence, that person might very well take the prison board's side, to the considerable embarrassment of the county administration.
5. Invite Strickland to undertake the overtime study with members of his staff. The court's administrative staff included several career professionals in court administration who were graduates of the Institute for Court Management.

They were undoubtedly capable of conducting the study, and Strickland and the prison board which he clearly dominated would certainly find them acceptable. The question again was one of objectivity. Truly favored this alternative, arguing that if, as he believed, they really were professionals, they would be objective. Kirby's response was insightful: "I don't recall chapter and verse but somewhere in the scripture it is written, 'Whose bread I eat, his song I sing,' and those fellows eat court bread."

Three things were essential: a dispassionate review of prison overtime usage, the development of sound recommendations that would reduce overtime expenses without endangering the public, and an appraisal of the adequacy of the current budgetary allocation for prison overtime. This last point was particularly important. Goodheart continually reminded the prison board that his overtime request had been cut arbitrarily by the finance department without consultation or even explanation. True, there were other important questions that the study could appropriately consider, such as the adequacy of entry-level salaries for correctional officers and the appropriateness of current staffing levels. But solutions to both of these problems would be likely to cost the county more money. Given a choice, Kirby would prefer to postpone consideration of all problems that might result in increased costs to the county until after the next election.

Fortunately, the collective bargaining agreement with the local union that represented the correctional officers was due to expire in September. The study would certainly be completed well before then, and any recommendations requiring work-rule changes could be negotiated as part of the contract settlement.

Kirby turned to Truly and said, "George, give this some thought—and quickly. See what you can come up with."

Truly knew he had to work fast to answer two questions: Which of the alternatives should be recommended? If a study were to be undertaken, what kind of expert should be given the assignment?

Discussion Questions

1. Judging from the statements and actions of the principal actors in the case, in what ways did their value premises differ?
2. What purposes, if any, are served by going on record, as Finance Director Dexter did in his first e-mail?
3. Instead of replying to Corrections Director Goodheart's memorandum of April 5 while he was still angry, what should Dexter have done?
4. Was Commission Chair Kirby correct in his observation that "writing is a very incomplete, very limited way to communicate"?
5. Kirby and County Administrator George Truly clearly have misgivings about the objectivity of a nationally recognized group of corrections experts. Are those reservations well founded? Would the recommendations of such a group be more likely to support or oppose the director of corrections? Why?
6. Which of the five alternatives—alone or in combination—should Truly recommend?
7. If the county administrator's recommendation involves a study, what kind of expert should be selected to head it? Should it be a member of the county staff or an outsider? Should partisan affiliation be a consideration? Should the prison board be consulted on the choice? How important is reputation in selecting a leader for such an assignment?
8. If a study is to be commissioned, what charge or instructions should be given to the analysts?

Suggested Simulation Roles

George Truly, county administrator
Jim Kirby, commission chair
Charles Goodheart, director of corrections
Don Dexter, finance director
Harvey Strickland, judge

For a larger role play:
Frank Friendly, personnel director
The six other commissioners

Part VI

Policy Implementation, Productivity, and Program Evaluation

Introduction to Part VI

Policy Implementation, Productivity, and Program Evaluation

A local government manager is ever attentive to the "big picture" processes of maintaining effective relationships with the governing body and the community, always behaving with integrity, and focusing on the future of the community. However, he or she must also worry about operational details. Some roles that accompany being the chief operating officer were addressed in the previous section, in the cases on human resource and budget management. Other aspects are addressed in Part VI and concern the manager's role in shaping and implementing the policy agenda.

The manager's first task in this area is to track and consider all information touching on policy issues and sort it into meaningful input for the council or board. Once elected officials have set the policy agenda, based on the input they receive from the manager and others, the manager then implements this agenda. This job is sometimes made more difficult when elected officials opt for a policy choice that the manager did not recommend or when the policy itself is not clearly defined.

Finally, the manager plays a retrospective role in monitoring the organization's success in carrying out policy directives and in evaluating the success of policies and procedures.

Part VI has two cases. Case 15, "Performance Measurement Sea Change," examines what happens when a community's government, under fiscal duress and facing allegations of impropriety, attempts to implement performance measurement. One might ask, "Why is this community concerned about performance measures when it has so many other problems?" but performance management is precisely the remedy prescribed by the electorate. The case illustrates the complexity of devising and installing a performance evaluation system when there is a paucity of data; a lack of enthusiasm in the departments; and an untried, inexperienced implementation team.

The second case, Case 16, "Contracting for Trash," allows us a look at the most basic of municipal services, solid waste collection, as well as the process of contracting with an external agency to provide a basic local service. The focus of the case is on finding the most cost-efficient and effective system for collecting residential trash. No issue generates more phone calls to elected officials than trash not picked up; no decisions evoke more NIMBYism (not in my backyard) than the siting of landfills and other waste-management facilities.

In addition to attending to the public's concerns, local governments must try to find space for landfills, modernize them to make the best use of compaction, and meet environmental standards that are increasingly more rigorous. One option is to contract the service to a private provider or even another local government. The bottom line of this case is how best to meet the "double E" standard of efficiency and effectiveness, rather than letting politics determine policy. One of the discussion questions requires some financial calculations, but the sidebar provides instructions on how to compute them.

The cases in Part VI cut across several management practice areas. These include policy facilitation, performance measurement, budgeting and financial analysis, human resource management, and even strategic planning.

15

Performance Measurement Sea Change

Kathryn Kloby

Background

Rockland is a large metropolitan city that is poised for positive change. Just taking a short walk along the riverfront and gazing at the cityscape reveals a glimpse of the city's rich history and recent transformation. A century ago Rockland's populace was almost double its current population of 200,000 residents. The post–World War II demographic and economic trends, paired with racial tensions during the civil rights movement, led many white residents to move into the suburbs, leaving behind African American and minority communities.

High-rises, once occupied by office workers and executives, and major department stores are either vacant or occupied by struggling small business and social service programs. Some of these art deco giants are being redeveloped as luxury apartments and condominiums. Steel and brick skeletons of former industrial sites lie dormant along the riverfront. However, an abandoned lace factory was recently demolished to make room for a gleaming, state-of-the-art sports arena that signals a new age of growth and prosperity to city residents and surrounding communities.

Revitalization faces many challenges. Violent crime is increasing. Schools are struggling to meet the needs of students but also the performance demands of state and federal mandates. Allegations of corruption have tarnished the reputations of the mayor, council members, and other appointed officials. Further, the city budget of $700 million has a projected shortfall of $150 million. Many consider mismanagement of city funds and lack of accountability for municipal operations to be the leading cause of the city's financial woes.

The recent election brought in a new mayor with fresh ideas and a new vision for the city. Mayor Mark Wilson's energizing speeches promise significant reforms in the business of government. Citizens want to see Mayor Wilson follow through on his campaign promises to create a safe and economically prosperous city that nurtures families. Thus all eyes are on this administration as it tries to systematically examine city resources and city service results so that it can make informed management and budget decisions. The pressure is on for the administration to show that it can make a difference, but newspaper headlines are highlighting a recent crime spree and the exorbitant costs of the new sports arena construction, and asking whether this mayor can deliver on his campaign promises.

To address the budget shortfall, the city under Mayor Wilson's leadership raises taxes and reduces its workforce of 5,000 by more than 400 city personnel. The workforce reduction entails some political risk because the city's unemployment rate is 9 percent—nearly double the state average—and the city itself is the largest employer in Rockland.

Indeed, critics of Mayor Wilson and supporters of the former mayor are taking actions to remove Wilson from office, claiming that he has shown minimal progress in his first months in office. The Committee to Recall Mayor Wilson is working to collect 32,000 signatures within 160 days so it can stage a special election. Mayor Wilson is not surprised by this resistance: the previous mayor had a charismatic style and connections to powerful individuals who helped him stay in elected office for several terms despite rumors of corruption.

Meanwhile, Mayor Wilson believes that building relationships with local leaders, educators, members of the business community, and residents is critical to his success in reforming the city's government. Early in his term, he established a transition team, whose several working committees would set key priorities for the administration in relation to the economy, education, public safety, government reform, and citizen concerns. The committees are populated by members of the business community, nonprofit directors, neighborhood representatives, pastors and leaders of faith-based organizations, and educators from local universities. Several committee meetings culminated in an extensive report with key strategic recommendations. The mayor is also filling the many empty seats on advisory boards aligned with key city functions.

To increase accountability to the public and improve management decision making, Mayor Wilson established the Office of Performance Management. OPM's mission is to institute a government-wide performance measurement and reporting system. A key goal of the system is to foster financial stewardship, with an emphasis on increasing revenue flows, reducing expenses, and improving asset management—all to improve program efficiency and effectiveness. Ultimately, the mayor wants this performance system to improve the quality of services and the quality of life for residents, and increase transparency. The mayor envisions OPM as a major conduit for reform.

After an extensive search, the mayor has hired Jordan Sanders to lead the Office of Performance Management. She has more than 15 years of private sector experience in marketing and project management. Her assignment is to lead the city into an age of increased accountability, with measurement and reporting techniques for ratcheting up performance. Provided with office space in the municipal building, authority to hire a team to take on this initiative, and the support of the mayor, Sanders hits the ground running. Her first job is to determine the scope of performance measurement across departments. Her aim is to show immediate and tangible benefits of the mayor's efforts, while instituting systemic changes to transform Rockland into a high-performing city.

In her initial weeks as the OPM director, Sanders interviews dozens of candidates and hired a team of six new staff. Two team members have extensive experience in private sector management and information technology. The other four are new to the field and appear hopeful and dedicated to the mission of OPM and the new mayor's initiatives.

Other experienced candidates declined Sanders's offer of a job, saying that the salary was not competitive. Sanders suspected as well that OPM's office space in city hall was a disappointment to several of the candidates. OPM staff share one large office rather than having cubicles or individual offices. Despite her limited resources, however, Sanders feels she has a good team ready to take on the new initiative.

Jordan Sanders's staff will meet frequently with department heads and their staff to design and implement performance measurement systems. She will also require all departments to submit monthly performance reports to OPM so that she can see what departments are measuring and how sophisticated their systems are. She plans to highlight successes for the mayor as well as areas in need of improvement. Having this bird's-eye view will help Sanders make informed recommendations on what the city needs to do to move forward. She is optimistic that she has the necessary resources, staff, and political support to bring performance management best practices to Rockland.

The Case

Eight weeks into the job, Sanders and her team are working feverishly to get the performance measurement on track. In her career, Sanders has never encountered as many challenges as she has faced in her first few weeks of employment in Rockland. As she sits at the head of the conference table looking at the expressions of her staff, she clearly sees that they, too, are feeling the strain. Sanders's weekly OPM meetings and daily interactions with her staff reveal several significant obstacles.

Clearly performance measurement is at a bare minimum across departments. Most departments rely on measures of inputs and outputs, but few department heads report that they use performance data to inform their decisions. Both inside and outside the city government, it is hard to understand what Rockland's tax dollars are accomplishing.

OPM's review of the newly mandated monthly departmental performance reports reveals little consistency in data collection or even technologies across departments. Some departments use Excel or Access, others use outdated software, and still others use paper-based methods for data collection and presentation. Sanders envisions a system that is fully integrated and consistent. At minimum, she aspires to standardized performance reports with data, targets, graphics, and a narrative that discusses performance achievements, shortfalls, and strategies for improvement.

Sanders had hoped that her vision of performance measurement would get personnel thinking and talking about ways to improve performance. After seeing the format of the performance reports that are being turned in, however, she realizes that it will take some time to change the way employees think about data and its connection to the outcome of the efforts of Rockland programs and departments. To many city employees, performance measurement is merely a tool for compliance rather than a way to inform decisions. Rather than asking, for example, "How can we improve performance?" they are more likely to tell OPM staff, "Just tell me what to do to get this new report done."

Sanders sees some glimmers of hope, however. One department head, John Hall, the newly appointed director of public works, is a shining example of how the OPM process and staff can be used by departments. He has met with OPM staff regularly to determine new performance indicators, timelines for introducing the new measures and data collection, and strategies for using the information to report to OPM and the public. His department collects data on the number of staff and their hours worked per week, the number of tons of garbage and recycling collected, the number of street miles resurfaced, and the number of sidewalk miles repaved.

Hall wants to introduce more indicators that document efficiencies and service quality, and he also wants to track citizen calls and complaints about matters such as snow removal, street repair, and abandoned cars. Since overtime hours have taxed his department's budget, he also wants help in monitoring worker productivity.

In addition, the finance department is making progress in monitoring and reporting revenues. Systems have been fine-tuned for timelier reporting of revenues generated via property tax collection, special tax collection, parking meters, and fees and permits. Also embracing the performance measurement initiative is the department of sanitation. It is starting to document key factors: complaints by type (for example, "illegal dumping," "no service," "street cleaning"); whether each complaint is addressed by the department; and the number of days that elapse before resolution.

However, the majority of department heads are frustrated by the extra demands of the new initiative. For example, the department of welfare, which provides job training and substance abuse programs for nearly 2,500 service recipients, tracks the number of active cases and the number of cases closed or on hold, as one might expect it to. However, it has little performance data to explain why cases are increasing or decreasing, the level of service quality, or ways to expedite the work of case managers. One welfare staff member described the confusion as "paralysis through analysis." The department's reports are data rich in terms of the number and status of cases, but they contribute little to informed decision making to improve services.

Given the resistance, for now Sanders and her staff are simply requesting department heads to select a few meaningful measures to track for their decision making, as a way to help the mayor with his forthcoming, 100-day report to the public on service accomplishments and the city's strategic direction.

While some departments are working through measurement challenges, a majority of department heads and staff have not warmed to the notion of collaborating with OPM to improve performance. The morale of city workers is at a critical low. Many feel alienated and even paranoid. Sanders blames the recent workforce reduction for this mindset. Her staff report that many city employees perceive the performance measurement effort as simply the latest way to finger underperformers. Others think Sanders's office is "out to get us." Still others simply cling to what they call "the old ways" of conducting the business of city government.

More often than not, OPM staff requests for meetings or monthly performance reports are ignored. Police and fire commissioners, for example, claim that uniform crime reports and response-time indicators tell the city everything it needs to know about crime and fire incidents. When Sanders made the mayor aware of this resistance, he told her to concentrate on the other departments, especially since the police department "has enough on its plate" with the recent spike in violent crimes.

Needless to add, Sanders's own morale is flagging. She senses that her team is considered a set of inexperienced outsiders with little authority. In many instances, OPM suggestions to refine data collection strategies are disregarded. OPM staff have resorted to working with any city employees willing to meet with them. In most cases, OPM staff have taken it upon themselves to design entirely new performance measurement systems as well as collect data and prepare monthly reports for departments. When Sanders leaves her office in the early evening hours, she does so knowing that members of her staff are likely to stay for several more hours to get their jobs done.

Sanders decides to bring in consultants who specialize in developing performance measurement systems. She hopes that these independent professionals will command more credibility than her staff seems to, so that city employees will finally see the value of the performance management process in a new light. The consultants are tasked with presenting a strategy to the OPM staff, holding several learning sessions across departments, and helping to establish a set of priorities and a streamlined process for measuring and reporting performance. Yet even her most enthusiastic staff members have misgivings after the preliminary meetings with the consultants. Some say the system the consultants propose is even more complex and cumbersome than the one they are trying to implement. Others wonder if the consultants will be able to design a system that is specialized enough to fit Rockland's needs.

Complicating the situation is the mayor's clear intent to find ways to include citizens in determining city priorities and identifying services in need of improvement. (Sanders has a constant reminder of the civic committees that met as part of the mayor's transition into office: a 900-page report stacked in her office.) Although she admires the mayor's willingness to engage the public, she also worries about the challenges of including the public in assessing the city's performance when progress to systematically measure and report on performance is going so slowly.

The Decision Problem

The new administration is three weeks away from Mayor Wilson's 100th day in office. Under pressure to show results, the mayor plans to recognize the milestone by delivering a progress report to citizens called the "100 Days Citizen Report." The report will be made available online, and the mayor will give a condensed version of the report at a ribbon-cutting ceremony for the new sports arena. He expects OPM to contribute a range of performance information from various departments.

The report will also outline priorities for the upcoming year. One priority is to find ways to include citizens in the governance process. In relation to Sanders's department, this priority means including citizen input in the performance assessment of city services. Ideas that are being considered include a citizen survey and working with neighborhood groups to determine citizen priorities and expectations of Rockland services.

When Sanders meets with the mayor to discuss his 100-day report, he reiterates his belief that citizen participation achieves transparency and enables citizens to interact more meaningfully with their city government. That way, he says, management decisions will be more reflective of citizen preferences and expectations. But as she listens to his ideas about citizen participation in assessing city services, she can't help but think of her staff working late into the night, of all of their efforts to meet with department heads, of the disgruntled look on employees' faces as they learn of yet another layer (that is, citizen input) to the performance measurement reform. Clearly, she needs to make some major decisions before the performance measurement initiative falls apart and a new, more citizen-focused initiative is planned.

On several occasions Sanders has briefed the mayor on the challenges of getting Rockland on a performance measurement track. She wants his explicit support for this initiative to show city staff that the performance measurement reform is not a passing fad. City employees need to understand that this performance measurement initiative is a marathon and not a sprint, she contends. She seeks a long-term commitment to develop a performance culture and system that can supply useful information for elected officials, administrators, and citizens.

After meeting with the mayor this morning, Sanders prioritizes the things she needs to address and frames these key questions:

- What information will she ask her staff to collect for the 100 Days Citizen Report?
- With regard to involving citizens in performance measurement, what should she propose to the mayor? Knowing little about citizen surveys and other collaborative approaches, whom should she consult to discuss realistic options?

The more pressing concern is OPM's contribution to the content of the 100 Days Citizen Report. Sanders realizes that it is just too soon to report on departmental performance, considering the lack of time she and her team have had to develop and implement the new system. On the second issue, she agrees that engaging citizens adds value to the initiative, but she did not expect this discussion so soon. In her mind, the difficulties associated with launching reforms and new initiatives, dealing with low staff morale, and developing new processes for data collection and reporting should all take precedence.

Sanders is scheduled to meet with Mayor Wilson again next week to debrief him on the accomplishments of OPM and its anticipated input on the citizen report. The meeting will be her opportunity to get the mayor's attention concerning the overall reception of the performance measurement reform. Sanders hopes that if the mayor is fully aware of the situation, their resulting decisions will convince all departments that the performance measurement reform is a long-term commitment that must be taken seriously. She has a lot to do before next week. During the walk back from the mayor's office, Sanders formulates her thoughts, takes a deep breath, and turns the corner into the OPM office.

Discussion Questions

1. What factors are hindering OPM Director Jordan Sanders and her team in reforming Rockland's performance measurement system?
2. Sanders's team has the dedication and energy to take on the challenge of building a performance measurement system. Yet several OPM staff are new to the field and even to the city. What is the effect of this lack of experience?
3. What is Mayor Wilson's role in performance measurement reform? What actions should he take to further the initiative?
4. What should Sanders and her team do to build support for performance management across departments?
5. Considering the limited measurement and reporting across departments, what types of information should appear in the mayor's report on his first 100 days in office?
6. How should Sanders address the mayor's eagerness to include citizens in Rockland's performance assessment? What strategy should she recommend for involving citizens in performance assessment?

Suggested Simulation Roles

Mark Wilson, mayor
Jordan Sanders, director, Office of Performance Management
John Hall, department head, public works
Six OPM staff members
Two or more performance measurement consultants

16

Contracting for Trash

Scott D. Lazenby

Background

The city of Newglade is located in a large metropolitan area and has a population of approximately 100,000. At the time the case unfolds, Newglade faced a problem with the collection of solid waste, or garbage. Communities in the metropolitan area used several different methods of collection, and Newglade found itself forced to evaluate its present collection system and to consider alternatives.

The case has the following cast:

Charles Veracruz, city manager

Chris Smith, assistant city manager

Thomas H. Moses Jr., new director of public works

Alfred E. Newhouse, budget director

Pat Chamber, administrative assistant, public works

Kay Hernandez, administrative assistant, finance

The case unfolds through the communication among these officials. The memo that launched the development of this case problem summarizes critical elements of the background.

CITY OF NEWGLADE
MEMORANDUM

DATE: May 2
TO: Charles Veracruz, City Manager
FROM: Pat Chamber, Administrative Assistant II
SUBJECT: Status of Residential Sanitation Operations

Per your request, this report provides information on the status of the residential sanitation operation.

Roughly 80 percent of Newglade's population is served by the city's curbside collection of an unlimited number of cans. (The other 20 percent of the population lives in apartments or other forms of housing that are served by the city's commercial sanitation operation.) Residential collection is twice a week, as mandated by the state—presumably to keep the fly population down. As you know, parks maintenance staff also collects uncontained waste or "loose trash" twice per month.

(continued)

The city has taken steps to reduce its garbage collection costs. The three-person rear-loading trucks were replaced with two-person manual side-loading packers. These in turn have been gradually replaced with one-person manual side-loaders. (The operator gets out of the cab to dump the garbage cans into the packer.) In spite of the city's average annual population growth of 10 percent, the sanitation staff has decreased from 43 (including supervisors) two years ago to 25 today (22 driver-loaders and 3 supervisors). No staff members were laid off; positions have been either vacated by normal attrition or transferred to other field operations.

The annual cost of operation is now approaching $2.7 million. Salaries and fringe benefit costs account for $1.7 million; vehicle maintenance and operation accounts for $434,000; landfill and waste disposal charges are $380,000; and lease-purchase payments on equipment are $79,000. These costs are covered in the general fund through taxes. Residents are not billed separately for sanitation service, although separate billing is the practice in some of the other cities in the metro area.

While the reduction in personnel has definitely lowered operating costs, the manual operation is not very efficient. The time taken by the driver to jump out of the cab and load the garbage cans adds to the time taken to complete a route. Of equal concern, the manual operation takes a physical toll on the driver-loaders. Last year there were twenty-two industrial insurance accidents that cost the city $32,400.

Field operations staff has done some preliminary investigation of automating residential collection (i.e., using trucks with equipment that picks up trash cans and dumps them mechanically into the truck), and we have reached the conclusion that this option should be pursued. Perhaps the new public works director will have some experience in this field.

Please feel free to contact me if you desire further information.

The Case

WHILE YOU WERE OUT

DATE: 5/3 TIME: 12:50
TO: CV
Mr. Tractar
Of: City Council called

Message: Said he was contacted by owner of Valley Waste Collection, who was upset that city doesn't contract out residential san. and doesn't allow private companies to provide commercial san. service in city. Call him ASAP.

RL

FROM THE DESK OF CHARLES J. VERACRUZ

5/3

Tom, here's a project to help you get your feet wet here! Could you and the public works staff look into contracting out residential garbage collection? There's some interest on the part of council.

CV

FROM THE DESK OF CHARLES J. VERACRUZ

5/3

Al, please have your budget staff do some analysis on the pros and cons of billing residents directly for garbage collection. Who pays for it now? What would we have to charge? How would this affect residents?

CV

Clipping file, *Los Diablos Times*, 6/14

NEWGLADE LOOKS AT SOCKING RESIDENTS FOR TRASH

NEWGLADE–In a workshop session Tuesday the Newglade City Council considered charging residents as much as $18 per month for collection of garbage.

Citing legal limitations on property taxes and political barriers to raising the sales tax rate, city staff proposed a sanitation "user fee" that would make garbage collection self-supporting and free up $2.7 million in general taxes now dedicated to trash collection.

Budget Director Alfred E. Newhouse stated that reducing general fund support for the residential sanitation operation would allow additional resources to be dedicated to police, fire, streets, and other critical city services. The garbage fee would be phased in over a period of several years, according to a staff report from City Manager Charles Veracruz. Collection service would remain the same under the proposal.

Veracruz also noted that the final rate could be as low as $11 per month, depending on cost-saving methods now being investigated by the city. The council took no action but referred the matter to the council budget committee.

CITY OF NEWGLADE
MEMORANDUM

DATE: June 21
TO: Charles Veracruz, City Manager
FROM: Al Newhouse, Budget Director
SUBJECT: Follow-up on Workshop on Garbage Fee

Given the circumstances, the press treated our report on the garbage user fee fairly kindly. One thing we didn't highlight in the report is the shift in tax burden that might result from the user fee. Here's some background:

As you know, the city uses several tax sources to fund sanitation and other city services. The most significant local tax is the 1 percent sales tax. This provides $23 million, or 37 percent of general fund revenues. Staff estimates that less than half of this is paid by local residents through normal retail purchases; the majority is paid by builders through their purchases of home and office building materials and by car buyers, many of whom come from neighboring cities to buy from Newglade dealers.

City property tax revenue for operations (i.e., excluding taxes levied for repayment of principal and interest on bonds) amounts to $5.0 million, only 8 percent of general fund revenues. The tax

(continued)

rate for residential property is $0.60 per $1,000 of value (0.6 mills) for the operating levy (the bond levy rate is an additional 0.5 mills). Commercial and industrial properties are taxed at 2.5 times this rate. State property tax limitations prevent the city from increasing the rate for the operating levy.

About 9 percent of revenue comes from development fees, utility franchise fees, and business licenses, and the remaining 46 percent comes from taxes that are collected by the state and distributed to cities on the basis of population.

While it certainly seems equitable to charge residents for service costs they incur, this does seem to shift the burden of funding from the commercial sector (and nonresidents) to the city residential sector. Further, the user fee can't be deducted for federal tax purposes, unlike some local taxes (notably the property tax).

According to economic theory, people make decisions based on how they would be affected financially. Therefore, the "economically rational" voter would oppose a fee that shifts costs away from businesses and would prefer a tax increase. Should we bring this up with the council?

On a related subject, our commercial sanitation operation more than pays for itself. The fund balance is at 50 percent of annual revenue, and the rates have been set lower than those of many of the surrounding cities in order to avoid building up an excessive balance. As a way of holding down the residential fee, we could combine the two operations into a single fund. Commercial sanitation could subsidize residential sanitation and still be competitive with rates charged by private companies for business garbage pickup.

* ELECTRONIC MAIL *

INBOX FOR USERNAME NEWHOUSE
FROM USERNAME: VERACRUZ
POSTED: JUNE 25/8:11:01 AM

Al, thanks for the follow-up report—shared it with the mayor last night. He said that "voters are rarely encumbered by concepts of economic rationality"!

CV

REPORT ON CONTRACTING FOR SANITATION SERVICES

JULY 6
Thomas H. Moses Jr., Director of Public Works
Pat Chamber, Administrative Assistant

At the direction of the city manager, the Public Works Department has completed an exhaustive and in-depth study of the merits and implications of contracting with the private sector for the provision of residential and commercial sanitation services. The background of this issue and staff recommendations are contained herein.

Commercial Sanitation

Cities use several methods for providing commercial sanitation services. In some areas commercial sanitation is unregulated, and each business is free to choose which private company it will

(continued)

use to collect its refuse. Some cities franchise one or more private haulers. Other cities, including Newglade, provide commercial sanitation as a municipal service, following the same philosophy as for the provision of sanitary sewer service.

Notwithstanding the fact that some larger cities divide their service area into several sectors for contracting out commercial sanitation services, it is felt that in an operating area the size of Newglade's, commercial sanitation can be provided most efficiently by a single operator. Moreover, if municipal overhead costs are kept low, the city will be able to compete effectively with the private sector, which must maintain sufficient rates to provide an adequate profit.

To contract for a service, the city must conduct a number of activities. It must draft, review, and advertise specifications. It must devise a selection process that weighs service quality against cost. It must review bids and check references. Following the award of a bid by the city council, the city must develop a service contract that protects the city against inadequate performance of the service. The contract should also include renewal provisions. Finally, the city must administer the contract, including inspecting the quality of the work, resolving service complaints, and providing contract payments.

Contracting out a service previously provided by the municipality has an impact on existing equipment and staff resources. In the case of commercial sanitation, a portion of the staff could be absorbed by other field operations. The successful bidder could also be required to offer jobs to city staff affected by the transition (although salary and benefit levels could not be guaranteed). The equipment would have to be sold; even if the contractor purchased the equipment, it would be at a depreciated value, thus reducing the city's assets.

The city uses service contracts in custodial and parks maintenance services. At one point, the city had to cancel the custodial contract because of poor performance at a cost to the city of $14,400 for a new contract. The higher administrative costs and potential loss of service quality are felt to be outweighed by the reduced labor cost inherent in the privately provided service.

Residential Sanitation

Provision of residential waste collection follows the same patterns as for commercial sanitation, except that municipal provision is more common for residential than for commercial sanitation. Service quality is of potentially greater political concern because of the considerable interaction between the service providers and residents-voters. Prompt and courteous service, including such things as careful handling of waste containers, is a critical component of municipal residential sanitation service.

* ELECTRONIC MAIL *

INBOX FOR USERNAME NEWHOUSE
FORWARDED BY USERNAME: VERACRUZ
POSTED: JULY 10/2:05:01 PM
FORWARDING COMMENT:

Al, Thought you might be interested in this message.

CV

(continued)

FORWARDED MESSAGE:
TO USERNAME: VERACRUZ
FROM USERNAME: MOSES
POSTED: JULY 10/11:51:20 AM

It has come to my attention that the budget director has proposed combining residential sanitation financing with the commercial sanitation fund. This is totally unacceptable. These must be kept separate to allow separate tracking by the operating managers and to avoid cross subsidies between the services. Charles, you must understand that I will not tolerate this kind of interference in the functioning of the Public Works Department.

–Thomas H. Moses Jr., Director of Public Works

The Decision Problem

CITY OF NEWGLADE MEMORANDUM

DATE: July 24
TO: Chris Smith, Assistant City Manager
FROM: Charles Veracruz, City Manager
SUBJECT: The Case Problem

Chris, I need your help in evaluating the city's options in residential sanitation. I will give you my file on the subject. Please see other staff as necessary to gather the information you need for your analysis.
Specifically, please analyze and give me your recommendations on the following:

1. Should the residential sanitation operation be automated? What would be the savings to the city in automating? Can you give me an idea of the payback period, net present value, or some other cost-benefit measure? If we do automate, should it be done at once or phased in over time? How would we handle the reduced staff needs?
2. As an alternative to automating, should we seek bids for contracting out the provision of residential sanitation services? Again, how would we handle the human resource issues? How would we guard against a decline in service?
3. Under either scenario, how should residential sanitation be financed—should we continue using general funds or establish a user fee? If the latter, should it be phased in? If user fees are initiated, should the residential and commercial operations be combined in a single fund?

Please summarize your conclusions in a memo that I could share with the mayor.

Meeting Notes, July 26

Meeting attendees: P. Chamber, K. Hernandez, C. Smith

Garbage collection assumptions:

Sixteen manual collection routes for the next two years (1 person per truck), with a route added every other year for population growth. Additional backup labor pool of 6 (to cover absences, training, etc.) for an initial total of 22 driver-collectors. 2.5 FTE supervisors (1 split with commercial san.). Automation would reduce initial routes to 13 and the backup labor pool to 5.

(continued)

Assume inflation factor of 5 percent per year.

Labor costs (including overtime, uniforms, etc.) are $53,200 per driver and $57,600 per supervisor. Add 30 percent for fringe benefit costs.

Assume workers' comp (industrial accident) insurance at current $32,400, proportional to number of drivers and inflation. Figure workers' comp will be one-quarter of this amount under automated system and also reduced in proportion to the reduction in drivers.

Both manual and automated trucks cost $160,000 each. The acquisition schedule for the current fleet of trucks is to replace two in one year, one in two years, two in three years, and so on at the rate of three trucks every two years. The current fleet could be sold for roughly $1 million total (assumes trucks have depreciated 50 percent on a straight-line basis and that the city would face a 20 percent price reduction in the used truck market).

New containers for the automated routes would cost $108 each. Would need enough for 80,000 population, assuming 3.5 people per household.

Vehicle operation and maintenance costs are now $434,000 and are assumed to be proportional to the number of routes and inflation.

A new fleet of automated trucks could be financed through a lease-purchase contract. Assume a 10-year term and 6 percent interest rate (annual payment is 0.14 times purchase price).

For net present value calculation, use a discount rate of 6 percent.

Discussion Questions

1. What should Assistant City Manager Chris Smith recommend to the city manager? Use the attached work sheet (Table 1) and the analytical methods described in the sidebar in this chapter to formulate a recommendation for the city manager. Here are steps to analyzing the cost of the two options. (You may find that entering the table into an Excel spreadsheet simplifies the computational tasks.)

Step 1. Complete the annual costs for the row labeled Total Manual System. Do the same for the row labeled Total Automated System before equipment. Then compute the total annual costs for the row labeled Total Automated System with new equipment. (Note that net equipment cost is computed. Add the annual lease/purchase cost to the labor and workers' comp cost to arrive at amounts for Total Automated System with new equipment.)

Step 2. Compute the row labeled Annual savings. Note this is the cost before investment in new equipment. Then compute the next row, Cumulative savings, which is a running total of the cost savings from automation.

Step 3. Compute the Simple payback period using the formula for uneven cost streams described in the sidebar.

Step 4. The next section involves computing the present value of the two options, the manual collection system and the automated collection system. Begin by completing the row labeled Net annual savings. This is the net savings from automation including the cost of the new equipment, both leased and purchased. Then compute the discount factor using the formula described in the sidebar. Assume a 6 percent discount rate for this problem. Then compute the row labeled

Table 1 Residential Sanitation Automation Worksheet

Prepared by C. Smith Date: August 6

	Year 1	Year 2	Year 3	Year 4	Year 5
MANUAL SYSTEM					
Labor costs:					
Inflation factor	1.00	1.05	1.10	1.16	1.22
# Routes	16	16	17	17	18
# Drivers	22	22	23	23	24
# Supervisors	2.50	2.50	2.50	2.50	2.50
Labor costs	$1,708,720	$1,794,156	$1,960,113	$2,058,118	$2,245,089
Workers' comp.	$32,400	$34,020	$37,345	$39,212	$42,963
Equipment costs:					
# Trucks purchased	2	1	2	1	2
Cost (x inflator)	$320,000	$168,000	$352,800	$185,220	$388,962
Vehicle O&M	434,000	455,700	508,390	533,810	593,471
Total Manual System					
AUTOMATED SYSTEM					
Labor costs:					
# Routes	13	13	14	14	14
# Drivers	18	18	19	19	19
# Supervisors	3	3	3	3	3
Labor costs	$1,432,080	$1,503,684	$1,655,117	$1,737,873	$1,824,767
Workers' comp.	$6,627	$6,959	$7,712	$8,098	$8,503
Total Automated System before equipment					
Equipment costs:					
# Trucks purchased	16				
Cost, new trucks	$2,560,000				
Salvage, manual trucks	$(1,000,000)				
New containers	$2,468,571				
Net equipment cost	$4,028,571				
Lease/purchase cost	$547,354	$547,354	$547,354	$547,354	$547,354
Total Automated System with new equipment					
Annual savings, automated system, before new equipment investment					
Annual savings					
Cumulative savings					
Simple payback period					
Net annual savings, including lease/purchase cost of new equipment					
Net annual savings					
Discount factor					
Discounted savings					
Net present value of savings					
PV of manual system					
PV of automated system					
NPV of savings					

Discounted savings by multiplying each of the net annual savings by the discount factor for that year. Sum the row to get net present value (NPV) of savings.

Step 5. An alternative approach is to compute the present value of the manual system costs, compute the present value of the automated system costs, sum the two rows, and compute the difference in the sums. This value should be the same as the NPV of savings found in step 4. In the event the city manager asks about the present value of the two options, you will have those figures readily available.

Two Simple Analytical Tools for Comparing Costs

For analyzing two or more options with different costs or benefits, finance analysts have developed several tools to identify the better option. One such tool is the payback period: the time (in years) that it takes to recoup the up-front investment costs of an option in future savings from lower operating costs. This up-front investment may be, for example, new equipment or facilities designed to lower future operating costs.

If the annual savings from the investment are uniform, then calculating the payback period is quite simple. For example, if an option to automate a particular activity costs $1 million up front in new equipment, and the expected annual savings from the automated process total $100,000 annually, then the payback period is 10 years.

If, however, the annual savings vary, then a few additional steps are needed to compute the payback period. First, compute the cumulative savings from the option with the up-front investment. Second, identify the year of payback in which the cumulative savings exceed the cost of the up-front investment (CumSavings). Third, use this formula to compute the payback period:

payback year − 1 + (net investment in equipment—CumSavings for year prior to payback year)/annual savings in payback year.

For example, if the automation option involves a $1 million up-front investment, and if annual savings double every year after the first year's savings of $100,000, then the payback period occurs in the fourth year.

Year	Annual Savings	Cumulative Savings
1	$100,000	$100,000
2	200,000	300,000
3	400,000	700,000
4	800,000	1,500,000

Using the above formula, the approximate point during the fourth year where the investment is recovered is computed as follows:

Payback period = 3 + (1,000,000 − 700,000)/800,000 = 3.375 years

The disadvantage of the payback period is that it does not account for the time value of money—*when* money is received or paid affects the relative advantage of an investment option. For example, an investment that provides quick returns will be highly preferable to one whose returns are delayed for a decade. Determining the present value of two or more competing options puts the comparison of their relative merits in the same time frame: the present. As such, the analysis will lead to choosing the more financially advantageous option without being biased by the timing of the costs (or net benefits) of the competing options.

To compute present value, the analyst must first decide on a discount rate—that is, the prevailing cost of capital in the marketplace at that point in time. The rate represents an opportunity cost to an investment decision. Next, the discount factor is computed using the present value formula:

(continued)

$$\frac{1}{(1+r)^n}$$

where r is the discount rate and n is the year in which the cost occurs. For a 6 percent discount rate, for example, the discount factor for costs (or savings) in the first year is

$$\frac{1}{(1+.06)^1} = 0.943396$$

These costs in year 1 are multiplied by the discount factor to get their present value (PV), or mathematically,

$$PV = \frac{1}{(1+r)^n} \times \text{Cost.}$$

This calculation is repeated for all years and for all options. The net present value (NPV) equals the difference in the sum of the costs for each option. The option with the lowest present value costs is the financially preferred one.

Robert L. Bland

2. City staff in Newglade analyzed the questions of automation and privatization simultaneously. Was this the best way to proceed, or should these issues have been addressed separately? Give reasons for your answer.
3. Was the mayor correct in his assessment that voters "are rarely encumbered by concepts of economic rationality" when considering tax and service fee questions? What role should these considerations play in the decision to be made here?
4. As the city manager, how would you have responded to the memo of July 10 in which the public works director opposed consideration of a merger of commercial and residential sanitation services? Would you include a combined system in your policy recommendation?
5. Under what circumstances would it be desirable to implement an automated collection system immediately? If such a change should be made, should the entire system be automated at once or gradually? What considerations factor into such a decision?
6. Questions of privatization involve both ideological preferences and objective, analytical considerations. List the ideological and analytical considerations. Under what circumstances should ideological considerations weigh more heavily than dispassionate analysis in making privatization decisions? What factors should weigh most heavily in this decision, and why?
7. How should long-run and short-run cost and savings considerations be weighted in this decision? Are elected officials and professional administrators likely to agree on the answer to this question? If not, how should administrators handle differences in perspective?

Suggested Simulation Roles

Chris Smith, assistant city manager
Staff assistant
Pat Chamber, administrative assistant for public works
Kay Hernandez, administrative assistant for finance

Part VII

Relating to Other Organizations

Introduction to Part VII

Relating to Other Organizations

Part VII, the final section of this book, reflects on the complexities that arise when an organization deals with other organizations, whether governmental or nongovernmental. Years ago, discussion of these complexities would center only on local-to-local relationships or a local government's subordinate or fiscal relationship to the state or the federal government. Today, nonprofit organizations and even private, for-profit organizations are part of the picture. Sometimes an international organization may even play a part in spite of the fact that local governments, constitutionally, do not engage in international relations. Instead of intergovernmental relations, today we speak of networks.

Case 17, "A Park, a School, and Two Strained Budgets," explores how two public entities, a school district and a municipality, go about negotiating one's desire to dispose of land and the other's desire to preserve a park. The community has limited open space for parks and has relied for years on a park maintained by the city but owned by the school district. However, faced with declining enrollments and revenues, the school district needs to sell the property. This case provides an excellent look at how two professional managers (a city manager and a school superintendent) work to negotiate a solution that is acceptable to both entities and to citizens.

Case 18, "The Manager's Role in Promoting Sustainability," looks at the manager's role in helping a struggling city find a path to sustained growth with emphasis on regional cooperation and environmental protection. With little experience in these areas, the manager's council is facing issues of conflict resolution, citizen involvement, strategic planning, and consideration of long-term sustainability. The case asks how fresh leadership can assist in finding a solution to long-standing decline. Sustainability is an approach that balances economic, environmental, and social interests in the development of public policies. ICMA is developing specialized leadership training to promote the concept.

The final case, Case 19, "A Jail in City Center," focuses on locating a corrections facility in an area that some citizens hoped would be an upscale city center. The all-too-frequent structural differences between cities and counties play a part in this case, but somehow two independent legal entities must reach a solution. The city administrator is cast in the role of broker to determine which interests will prevail—the city's desire for economic development or the county's need for a public safety facility. Potential ethical snags abound.

The cases in Part VII deal with a number of management practices such as policy facilitation, functional and operational expertise and planning, citizen service, initiative, risk taking, vision, creativity, and innovation. The reader also will see elements of democratic advocacy, budgeting, strategic planning, and media relations.

17

A Park, a School, and Two Strained Budgets

Gary L. Sears

Background

A key challenge that most local government administrators face is negotiating with other public bodies over the use or development of community resources. This case is based on the desire of the Central City School Board to close a school and adjacent park and use the proceeds from the sale to improve other school facilities and programs.

Central City has maintained the park for the school district since the 1950s, when it was dedicated to the schools as part of an area-development plan. Because the park has become integral to the city's open space as well as its recreational programs, the elected members of both boards know that the potential sale of the park could affect the outcome of the next election. This case is about the alternatives that the staff and governing boards develop to use tax dollars wisely to benefit the community at large.

Central City is a small, suburban, first-tier city making plans for its 2010 centennial celebration. It is adjacent to a large metropolitan community. Central City has a council-manager form of government, with seven council members and a mayor who is selected from the council. Four council members are facing reelection in the fall. Newspaper articles and discussions at budget meetings often concern the cost of acquiring the park, given that city revenues are declining.

Because the city is landlocked and predominantly residential, the residents highly value parks and open-space improvements. City council members know that the preservation of an open area near a residential area is crucial to the quality of life in the community. Most residents like living in Central City because it is close to a major university and features many recreational opportunities in the immediate area. There are several environmental groups in Central City, such as the city-appointed Keep Central City Green Commission. The park in question has a historic importance because of its old cherry grove, which predates the city's incorporation. They strongly support its preservation as an important part of the open space and character of the community.

From a financial viewpoint, spending city money to buy the park from the school district is problematic. The city's regional shopping mall, which once provided nearly 50 percent of the city's income (from sales taxes), recently closed because of competition from newer malls. Most building sites that otherwise would be available for new development in Central City are brownfields, and so the city council and manager know that redeveloping these sites will be costly and time-consuming. The likelihood is remote that any new development will deliver sufficient tax revenues to assist the city in buying the park. To complicate the situation, voters recently defeated a proposed increase in the city's sales tax rate, forcing the city to make major cutbacks in services, including laying off employees.

Meanwhile, the school district is suffering from declining enrollment, as many families in Central City send their students to schools in neighboring jurisdictions, where the schools are better funded and able to offer more services. Because the state distributes funds to school districts based on current enrollment, the loss of state funding due to its declining enrollment has forced the district to close two schools. In addition, as a small, landlocked school district which cannot expand its boundaries, and with no prospects for automatically increasing its school enrollment based on geographical growth, the district has had to neglect or postpone important repair and maintenance for its school facilities. Severe financial setbacks are also compromising after-school programs, school safety, and plans to attract new students. School board members thus view the potential sale of Cherry Grove Park as a means to get cash to improve school services, carry out needed capital projects, improve teacher pay, and attract new students to the school district.

Cherry Grove Park

The four-acre Cherry Grove Park is all that remains of the cherry orchard, which was mostly lost to development in the 1950s (see Figure 1). The developer dedicated the park to the school district to meet the open-space requirements of the city, and the district built an elementary school on a portion of the park site. However, in the early 1980s the school district abandoned the school and leased it to a private elementary school, the Cherry Grove Learning Center, which now pays $15,000 annually for the lease.

Figure 1 Map of Cherry Grove Park and the Surrounding Area

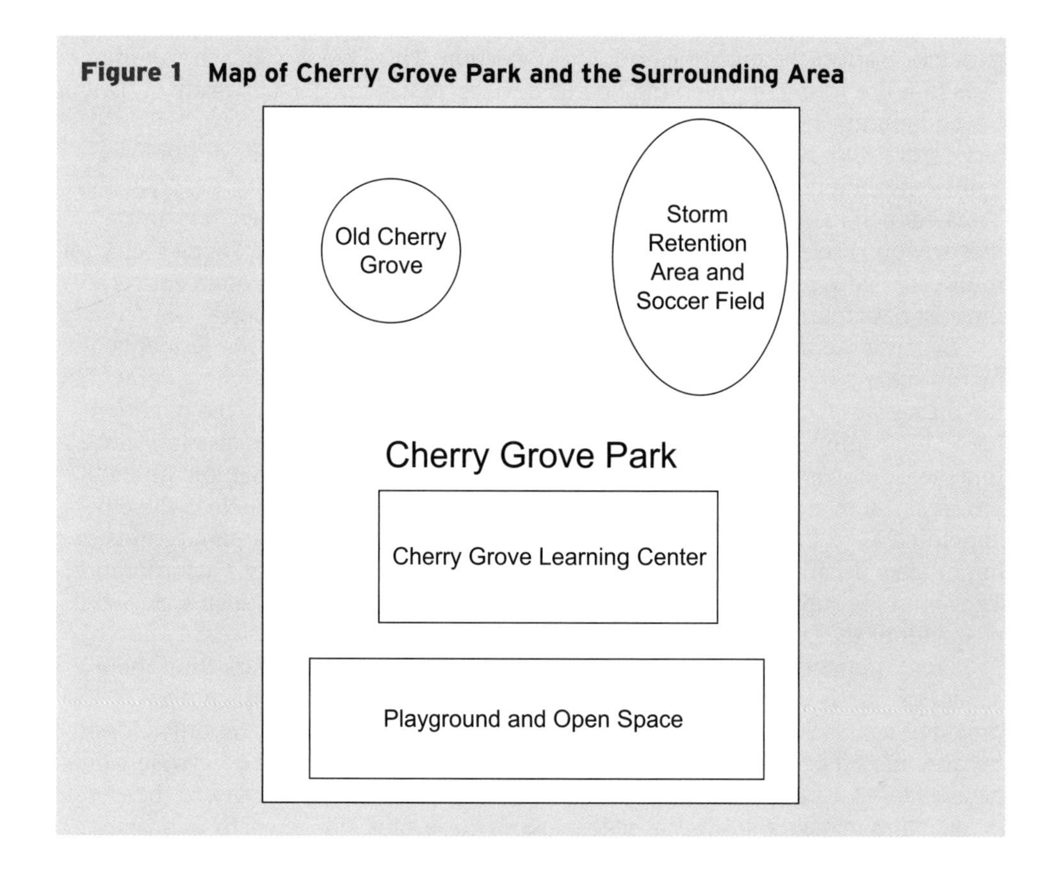

Because of pressing infrastructure needs elsewhere in the district, the school district has declared Cherry Grove to be surplus property. It gave the city formal notice that it was planning to sell both the school and the park and that it would develop a request for proposal to identify a real estate firm to market both properties. Even though the city has maintained the park for many years, there has never been a cost-sharing or use arrangement between Central City and the school district. Under the original dedication agreement and title for the park, the school board is required only to give the city notice of its desire to sell the property.

During the years that the school district has owned the property, the park has been a popular place for family gatherings, company picnics, and a host of community events. In addition to open space, the park offers playgrounds, shelters, soccer fields, and a dog park. The Cherry Grove Learning Center is also an important part of the community; many residents send their children to the school.

The Case

Upon hearing that the school district had declared the property to be surplus, Cherry Grove Park neighbors began calling city council members, school board members, and key staff members to insist that it was "absolutely critical to keep the park as a park." The residents circulated petitions and began showing up at council meetings and school board meetings, pleading that the two boards cooperate so that the park would not have to be sold to a private developer. Soccer players, animal advocates, and Cherry Grove Learning Center teachers and students all attended one meeting, demanding that the two governing boards preserve the park. As the meetings grew more heated, several residents threatened a recall, saying that the existing members would not be retained in the fall election if the two boards did not preserve the park.

At the public meetings, several city council members expressed dismay at the school board's decision to sell the property without first contacting the city. Meanwhile, school board members noted, at their public meetings, that the school district's desperately needed improvements outweighed the use of a park by a few residents. Because Cherry Grove Park serves both residents and people living outside the city's borders, several school board members commented that at least the funds from the sale of the property would be spent within the community.

The relationship between the school district board and the city council has been outwardly cordial, but the local newspaper has run letters to the editor from residents attacking both boards for failing to look at the benefits of preserving the park. An article pointed out that many residents who purchased their homes adjacent to the Cherry Grove Park did so because of the open space it provided to the neighborhood. These homeowners contended that the loss of the park would severely reduce the value of their homes and the quality of life in the community.

Several council members have publicly criticized the long history of city funds being used to supplement and subsidize school programs such as parks and recreation activities, school-bus maintenance, and school police officers. Some city council members, observing that the school district had not paid to maintain Cherry Grove Park for over thirty years, questioned why any city tax dollars should be used to acquire the park.

For their part, the school board members were feeling the pressure from recent school district layoffs and the need to improve school facilities. Many of them were convinced that the future of the school district itself was contingent on the sale of Cherry Grove Park.

Early in the negotiations, the city manager had several meetings with the school superintendent, but they arrived at no acceptable compromise.

The Negotiating Committee

Faced with increasing pressure to come to terms on the sale of the property, the two governing boards formed a negotiating committee. Despite their different missions, both boards had confidence in both the superintendent and the city manager, and most of the elected officials on the committee believed that their staffs could come up with an acceptable compromise. The formation of the negotiating committee engendered a collective feeling that the discussions were finally moving in the right direction, even though negotiations were likely to remain contentious.

This negotiating committee consisted of two representatives from the school board, two from the city council, the school superintendent, and the city manager. The committee's task was to explore the alternatives for the park's future and report to the two boards about proposed terms for a sale.

Because the negotiating committee's first meeting was framed as a "real estate discussion," attorneys for the school board and the city ruled that it could be held in executive session, without the news media present. However, the final decision would go to both boards in open session for approval. While many of the key elements were discussed behind closed doors, others, such as the appraisals, were ruled to be public, and the terms of the appraisals were to be made available to the community and the local newspaper.

The local reporter assigned to the story was angry about his exclusion from the negotiating sessions, proclaiming that the First Amendment allowed him to be at the meetings because public funds were involved in the disposition of the park. However, both sides' attorneys maintained that only the final contract would need to be discussed in public, and that position held.

In preparation for these meetings, the city council and the school board arranged for their respective appraisals of the park and the school site. The city council asked the city manager and staff to review the budget to determine sources of revenue for acquiring the site. After consulting the directors of finance, public works, and parks and recreation, the city manager presented several potential sources of funds to the city council and the negotiating committee.

Potential Sources of City Funds

A list of potential funding sources is shown in the sidebar on the next page. These sources include the following:

Capital Improvement Fund

The capital improvement fund consists of proceeds from one-half cent of the city's 3.5 cents per $1.00 sales tax. The fund can be used to pay for land acquisition, building upgrades, and (generally) all expenditures over $5,000. City staff calculated that nearly $250,000 of the fund could be used for the park's acquisition, but doing so would mean delaying other important projects, such as major street improvements; new police, public works, and fire vehicles; municipal building repairs; new street lights; a police building "facelift"; and purchase of emergency management communications equipment.

General Fund

A portion of the unrestricted reserves in the city's general fund could be used, but the reserves were recently reduced to approximately $3 million, or 10 percent of the general fund's annual expenditures. The city auditors recommended against further reductions in the reserves—they were needed as a cushion to prevent more layoffs or service cutbacks. A lower balance would also put the city's bond rating in

Cherry Grove Park Appraisals and Funding Alternatives

Appraisals

City of Central City, October 2006: $1.4 million—$5.50 per square foot
Cherry Grove School District, January 2007: $1.2 million—$5.25 per square foot

City Funding Alternatives

1. Capital improvement funds—up to $250,000.
2. General fund reserves—up to $3 million. However, any reduction would take reserves below the city auditors' recommended 10 percent of estimated revenues.
3. Conservation land payments (lottery funds). Reallocate funds from needed projects up to $250,000, which is the estimated annual revenue.
4. Open-space tax and grants. The city receives about $50,000 per year from this new county tax. It can pursue additional grants for up to $250,000 per year for open-space acquisitions.

jeopardy. Last, because the city's revenues were declining, tapping into the reserves could jeopardize the city's ability to meet the state's balanced budget requirements.

Conservation Land Payments

The city started getting conservation land payments from state lottery proceeds three years ago. These payments amount to approximately $250,000 for each fiscal year. However, they are already dedicated to a park shelter, golf course renovation, capital equipment, and other expenditures in the parks master plan, which was approved when the funds first began to roll in.

Open-Space Tax and Grants

The county voters approved an open-space tax, consisting of one-fourth of 1 percent of the county's sales taxes. First levied last year, the county tax makes possible a rebate to municipalities, based on their population. Central City's share is about $50,000 per year. Also, the county distributes 50 percent of the county's share of the funds to its member jurisdictions for open-space projects.

The city could apply annually for grants from this fund for acquisition of the park or open space, but the awards are highly competitive. No jurisdiction has received more than $250,000 in any calendar year from this grant program, and the city would be required to put up a 10 percent match for any funds received. Furthermore, these funds cannot be used to improve buildings; they are only for acquisition or improvement of open space.

Appraisals of the Cherry Grove Property

As the city continued to review sources of funding for acquisition of the park, the city and the school district received their respective appraisals.

The city's appraiser delivered his report to the city manager, staff, and negotiating committee in early October, appraising the property at $1.4 million, or approximately $5.50 per square foot. The appraiser had a hard time finding comparable properties that had sold recently. Most comparable properties were open-space sites in neighboring communities, and their values were not comparable to the value of a park and a school. The city preferred that the appraisal include only similar public spaces, but the appraiser's report also included developable open space, which raised the appraised value of the property.

In early January, the school district received its appraisal, which to the surprise of both parties came in at approximately $1.2 million—not quite $5.25 per square foot and $200,000 below the city's appraisal. At the next negotiating meeting, it was clear that the city would have preferred a much lower appraisal and the school district would have preferred a much higher one. The negotiating committee members asked the appraisers to confer on whether they could agree on a compromise value for the land.

In the appraisers' discussions, the city appraiser learned that the school district's appraiser used only open space in suburban areas, including some rural and undeveloped land, instead of developable land in an established community, which was the primary basis for the city's appraisal. The school district's appraisal was also lower because it took into account storm drainage improvements that would be needed if the park were to be developed. Ultimately, the appraisers agreed that a compromise figure would be acceptable, given that both their appraisals lacked comparable, recently sold properties.

As the negotiations continued, citizens kept up their lobbying of both the school board and the city council to retain the park as part of the community's open space. An aggressive action group supporting the park began to write letters to the editor and show up at board meetings, expressing their anger at being shut out of the negotiating sessions and demanding that the park be kept a park. Both boards felt pressure to forge a financial agreement to resolve the issue before the election.

Dividing the Property and Funding Alternatives

The appraisers had compromised on a value of $1.3 million, but the school superintendent and members of the school board now pressed the city for immediate payment for the property because of the urgent needs of the school district. However, because it also was cash strapped, the city's aim was to negotiate purchase of the property over a period of years.

Independently, the school board invited several real estate agents to give it proposals to buy the property. Discussions ensued about breaking the property into three parcels, with (1) the city buying a smaller parcel for open space and a storm drainage area, (2) the Cherry Grove Learning Center buying a second portion of the property over time, and (3) the school district selling the third piece of the property for real estate development.

School board representatives discussed this idea at a school board meeting before taking it to the negotiating committee. Property owners near the park were outraged and circulated petitions to recall any council member or school board member who supported the plan. The homeowners group then decided to sue the city for failure to follow its park master plan, which was predicated on the importance of open space and preservation of parks. (The plan indicates that the nearest park to Cherry Grove Park is almost two miles away.)

The negotiating committee requested that the city manager and school superintendent identify alternatives for resolving the park issue.

City Alternatives

The city's four best alternatives were these:

1. Do nothing, allowing the school district to sell Cherry Grove Park and the Cherry Grove Learning Center.
2. Pay the compromise price for the park ($1.3 million) using open-space funds, lottery funds, general fund reserves, and any other available funds to buy

the entire site (including the school). In this scenario, the city would need to negotiate a new lease with the Cherry Grove Learning Center or, if the city used open-space grants, relocate the school.

3. Buy the site from the school district but (a) pay a higher rate, requiring the school district to demolish and relocate the Cherry Grove Learning Center if required by open-space grants, or (b) exclude the Cherry Grove Learning Center from the agreement and pay a lower rate to the school district, since the school district will continue to receive payments from the center.
4. Divide the property into the three parcels proposed by the school board, with the city buying only the northern piece (see Figure 1) for parks and drainage requirements.

School Alternatives

The school district's four best alternatives were these:

1. Stop negotiating with the city, ignore the public pressure, and use a request-for-proposal process to sell the property to the highest and best bidder.
2. Accept the $1.3 million (compromised appraisal amount) for the park and school over time and continue to lease the school site.
3. Accept the lower appraisal amount of $1.2 million and agree to timed payments, but require the city to take responsibility for any demolition or relocation costs for the Cherry Grove Learning Center.
4. Require the city to pay the higher appraisal of $1.4 million, and have the city take over the relocation of the school, if such is required in the open-space grants.

What To Do?

Consideration of these alternatives polarized the negotiating committee. The mayor and the school district superintendent met on the issue as well, but as policy leaders they were reluctant to compromise on their earlier pledges regarding the future of the district and the city.

Despite the contentious negotiations, however, the city manager and school superintendent knew that the integrity of their institutions could be preserved if they arrived at a creative, workable solution. This willingness to compromise led to a plan they thought would satisfy the objectives of both governing boards.

They presented their plan to the negotiating committee and gained its support. The committee then asked them to present it to both governing boards in public, so that the surrounding property owners, private school officials and parents, and news media could attend.

Discussion Questions

1. What do you think the elements of the compromise plan were?
2. Why would the city be willing to accept the plan?
3. Why would the school district be willing to accept the plan?
4. What types of individuals (elected officials, staff) should be on a negotiating committee? Why?
5. What criteria should apply to selling public assets? Should there be a public referendum to decide whether the park will be preserved or sold for development?

6. Should there be more community involvement in the decision? If so, at what point should individuals or groups have been invited to participate in the decision making—and in what ways?
7. Should public agencies let local interest groups affect a decision to sell a public property?
8. What other alternatives would you consider?
9. Would there have been a better way to resolve this issue than that described in this case study?
10. Because both entities are funded by taxpayers, should the school board simply transfer the property to the city at no additional cost to the taxpayers?

Suggested Simulation Roles

City manager
School district superintendent
Members of the boards and negotiating committee
Community member
Homeowner living adjacent to the park
Taxpayer supporting the school district's selling the property
Taxpayer opposing the city's buying the property
Appraiser
Parks and recreation director
Finance director
Other staff member
Private school leader

18

The Manager's Role in Promoting Sustainability

Ellen Szarleta-Yancy

Background

After more than 50 years of reliance on heavy industry to sustain its population, the city of Stillville is facing the challenge of urban blight and all its associated problems. The city needs to move in a new direction.

Stillville is the second-largest city in the state, with a population of just under 100,000 people. Located on a major waterway, from the 1940s through the 1970s it was the hub of economic and social activity for Northside County and the surrounding three-county region. However, the exodus to the suburbs left the city with decaying infrastructure and the environmental legacy of uncontrolled use of vital natural resources. Along with these losses, the city suffers from old-style politics and the social consequences of a long history of isolation, both enforced and self-imposed.

During the years of its prosperity, Stillville attracted a large number of eastern and southern European immigrants. Employment opportunities also brought immigrants from Mexico and blacks from the southern reaches of the United States.

The diverse character of the population created both opportunities and challenges. Assimilation of European immigrants was pursued aggressively here as it was in other Rust Belt localities, but, as in other Rust Belt localities, their assimilation was associated with problems including discrimination, segregation, and the concentration of political power.

Initially, political power resided in the hands of a few white males who led the charge for economic growth. Over time, the political machine was built on the votes of the immigrant population. Jobs and benefits went to those who supported the ruling politicians and fueled the political machine. Political corruption was expected, largely tolerated, and thriving because loyalty brought economic benefits. However, the division along ethnic and racial lines provided little room for African Americans and Mexicans to participate and, as a result, they were largely isolated and marginalized.

Then the social transformation occurring nationwide in the 1960s and the large-scale automation of industrial processes eliminated 80 percent of the city's manufacturing jobs. Once a city supported by industry and able to support its residents, Stillville began to suffer from industrial closures, increasing unemployment, and rising ethnic tensions. Economic devastation was accompanied by a growing political vacuum.

Today, the city sustains a couple of large-scale manufacturing plants and is using its environmental assets to promote tourism. For example, the lakes that long served industry also gained recognition as recreational outlets, even thought that was not anticipated in the original design of the city. Now efforts are underway to renew the few existing parks and recreation areas, and a vision has been formulated for expanding the lakefront as a tourist destination.

At the center of the tourism initiative since the 1990s is an industry relied on by many cities in similar situations: gambling. City and state leaders initially hoped that gambling would encourage tourism, spur economic development, and move the city forward in a relatively short time. The large population base of surrounding communities would provide consumers from "external" markets. In addition, close proximity to major airports and transportation centers could mean an influx of destination gamblers and tourists.

However, visitors to the city have alternatives to gambling in the form of recreational sports and cultural events in the renovated convention center. Moreover, the larger region is supported by and supports the city in important ways. Surrounding communities offer a host of options ranging from nature hikes to shopping, and visitors see the assets of nearby communities as an important attraction. However, the city has made little effort to work collaboratively with its neighbors.

Economic initiatives over the past twenty years have been piecemeal. Without a long-term plan, the direction of the city's efforts has changed with each mayor. Each new mayor spotlighted a "showcase" for his term, and these projects were undertaken and completed with limited support from the city council. Citizens at large were not invited to participate in defining the new Stillville.

Meanwhile, other communities in the region have been moving forward with coordinated plans to revitalize economically, socially, and environmentally. So while newer communities engage in visioning programs, Stillville is being left behind.

Recognizing the city's current status is not the problem: whether talking to residents on the streets or representatives of the city, one hears the same litany. The larger problem is deciding on the city's future direction, and then implementing policies that support the vision.

This problem now belongs to Richard Domore, the new city manager, along with the city council and Mayor Mark Myturn. Another new player on the scene is the Regional Excellence Initiative (REXI) Executive Committee, which recently released an important sustainable development proposal that will affect Stillville.

Richard Domore, City Manager

Richard Domore came to Stillville with more than ten years of city management experience. He had been manager for two suburban communities of fewer than 3,000 residents each. Aware of the mounting challenges faced by Stillville, he nevertheless came on board with enthusiasm at the prospect of applying his training and experience in an urban setting.

When Domore interviewed for the position, the council probed his views on the importance of developing trust in city government and fostering interdepartmental collaboration. Their concern focused on a long-standing turf war between the city's department of environmental affairs and department of economic development. This turf dispute was seriously impeding communication between the city staff and the council members on important growth issues. The previous city manager exerted no leadership in solving this problem.

However, since taking the city manager position six months ago, Domore has met with individual department heads, established interdepartmental committees, and conducted collaboration training sessions for all staff members—all with the support of the city council. These initiatives have built a foundation for trust among employees and departments, and the focus internally is beginning to change for the better. Employees now are less concerned about turf, in the sense of which department has responsibility for an initiative, and they are more focused on outcomes: what progress can be shown as a product of the collaboration.

City Council

The city council is composed of seven members: two at-large representatives and five members representing districts. One of the council members serves as president, while the chief executive for the city is the independently elected mayor. For a long time, political insiders maintained their elected positions by relying on the political machine. Long-established loyalties cemented voter commitment to those representatives who sought to protect the city's interests—albeit at the expense of good relationships with the surrounding communities. Partisan elections and low voter turnout worked against modernizing local politics, although a recent influx of younger residents, many of them white-collar professionals, offers some hope for change. In fact, in the last twenty years, the council's composition has included more women and younger members with a broader vision of the city's interests. The current council president is now in his fourth term as an at-large member and his third term as president. Of the remaining members of the council, four are in their third terms, and two are newly elected.

For the past five years, the distribution of casino revenues has topped the council's agenda. Monies went to infrastructure development such as street and sidewalk repair, renovation to convention facilities, a senior citizens' center, and the construction of new city buildings. The council has considered areas for economic revitalization but has not revisited the city's master plan or the zoning ordinances in over ten years. Transportation concerns have also been neglected.

However, since Richard Domore was hired as city manager, the pace and the direction of change have overwhelmed the city council. Instead of reviewing relatively routine matters, as it has for the past ten or twenty years, the council is finding itself confronted with new policy issues suggested by the manager and supported by younger residents. Previously the council members were able to call directly on department heads for clarification on projects of interest, and they could easily identify which department had project responsibilities. Accountability was simple, and budget allocations could be adjusted on a system of rewards and punishments. Domore's approach, however, is interdepartmental, and he emphasizes economic development in the context of environmental issues, while enforcing the council's responsibility to deal with the city manager, not the staff. Accountability, as the council has always viewed it, is more difficult to discern now.

When the council hired Domore, it simply wanted the two problem departments—environmental affairs and economic development—to get along, both to expedite street and park improvements and to bring new businesses to the area. Citizens were agitating to see progress that benefited the individual citizen. Now, with the change in departmental relations, the council must rely more on the expertise of Domore. They still believe they made the right choice in hiring him, but they had not expected the challenges of his broader vision.

One clear adversary is Tom Whitco, the council president. The shift in power is making him uncomfortable. Change is occurring too quickly under Domore and he wants to slow it down. Furthermore, Whitco sees that Domore and the mayor share policy interests and positions that are contrary to his own—specifically their interest in regional sustainable development. Whitco believes in self-reliance and sound economic development planning. "Local economic development should be performed by the locals. The natural environment is our strongest economic resource," he says.

Mark Myturn, Mayor

The election of Mark Myturn three years ago was a stunning upset. His opponent, Sam Simon, is a prominent, long-standing member of the opposing party. Not only is Simon a party leader but he also is a prominent businessman serving the largest manufacturing facility in Stillville and, previously, serving the city itself. Simon and Whitco are close friends.

Myturn's success was attributed to his message of change. A professional manager by training, he maintains that economic development can benefit the community only if it focuses on the long-run interests of the community. He wants the city to create a vision for itself that will address the issues of crime and poverty, ecological sustainability, and business growth simultaneously—in other words, he seeks sustainable development.

The Corporations

International Manufacturing Corporation and World Business Corporation are the city's two largest employers. IMC is an international manufacturing operation and employs more than 5,000 people. WBC, also worldwide, has multiple interests. In the city of Stillville, it employs almost 4,000 workers in tourism-related enterprises. Both companies rely on easy access to major transportation routes including ports, roads, and airways.

IMC uses the ports and roads to transport both raw materials used in manufacturing processes and the resulting products. Congestion occurring on major transportation routes as a result of suburban sprawl and the resulting accidents and road hazards have caused IMC to miss some contract deadlines. IMC realizes that the region has experienced growth overall, especially along transportation routes, and that citizens are becoming frustrated by the high level of industrial truck traffic.

However, the city, region, and state would be significantly less prosperous without IMC's presence. In fact, IMC plans to expand its manufacturing and is finalizing design plans for another plant in the city that will employ an additional 400 people. The expansion is expected to increase the property tax payments made to the city by more than $2 million.

Growth is essential to long-term profitability—although not without cost to the community. A legacy of the area's long industrial history is high levels of both air and water pollution. While in compliance with federal and state regulations, IMC knows that any proposal to increase the size of its plants will not get a favorable reception from environmentalists because of the resulting increase in emissions.

WBC is a relative newcomer to the region. It also relies on diverse transportation modes for its various enterprises. Tourists arrive by road and air, and materials and supplies are delivered via port access and truck delivery. The growth potential of the firm and the tourism industry is heavily dependent on safe, reliable, and easy access to transportation. As concerns heighten regarding gas prices and energy efficiency, WBC would like to see reasonably priced transportation alternatives in the region.

WBC also sees growth potential in the city and the region. As the region's population continues to grow, WBC will draw new customers to its tourism-based facilities, even if they do not gamble. It is planning for growth in the restaurant and hotel sectors. The hospitality industry will require higher levels of disposable income, and it must market the city as a destination. The image that tourists want to see is one of clear blue skies, long stretches of clean lake beaches, and appealing entertainment and restaurant venues—no reminders of issues they face in their own hometowns. For Stillville to become a true national destination, it will have to acquire new shoreline property, construct at least one large hotel and convention center, and build more access roads.

The Case

REXI and the Regional Planning Commission

Approximately twenty years ago, the state legislature established a regional planning commission for a three-county area. The Regional Planning Commission (RPC) is responsible for transportation planning and, to a lesser extent, economic development planning in the Stillville area. RPC's mission is to improve the long-term economic, social, and environmental conditions of the three-county region, but resources have been limited and transportation planning has taken priority. Although it lacks binding authority on individual cities and towns, the commission has earned a reputation for providing excellent services and advice.

The Regional Excellence Initiative (REXI) is a product of the RPC and is housed in the RPC. It was formed five years ago, when concern for a more balanced approach to development emerged in the region. An executive committee formulates resolutions to guide cities and towns in their quest for sustainable development and presents them to the full REXI board. Recently, the REXI board unanimously endorsed Resolution 101 (see Exhibit 1).

REXI's seven-member executive committee represents the interests of the three member counties. The mayor (or a designated appointee) of the largest city in each

Exhibit 1

PLANNING COMMISSION RESOLUTION NO. 101-LRPC

ADOPTED SEPTEMBER 22, 2008
SUSTAINABLE DEVELOPMENT FOR THE FUTURE
ENVIRONMENTAL QUALITY PLAN—PART ONE

WHEREAS the Regional Excellence Initiative Board of the Regional Planning Commission held a public hearing on September 22, 2008, to consider the Sustainable Development for the Future—Environmental Quality Plan—Part One; and

WHEREAS the three-county region has effectively been designated by the U.S. Environmental Protection Agency as an air nonattainment area for more than ten years; and

WHEREAS the growth projected for the region over the next twenty years will require additional roads and more vehicle-miles traveled; and

WHEREAS the focus of RPC must shift from one of developing new transportation routes and expanding road systems to one of investing in regional transit systems; and

WHEREAS continued industrial growth, with increased air and water emissions, will limit an improvement in human health conditions and the natural environment,

BE IT FURTHER RESOLVED that by adoption of this resolution, the Regional Excellence Initiative endorses and supports the following actions.

1. A moratorium on the facility expansion will apply to the three largest industrial facilities in the three-county region for a period of at least three years.
2. A regional transportation network will be created, consolidating all existing city and town systems and providing service to new areas. The transportation hub will be placed in the city of Stillville, in Northside County.

PASSED AND ADOPTED BY THE REGIONAL EXCELLENCE INITIATIVE, OF THE REGIONAL PLANNING COMMISSION THIS 22ND OF SEPTEMBER 2008.

county is a voting member of the committee, along with four at-large representatives. When Mayor Myturn took office, he appointed Jane Environ, the head of the environmental affairs department, to be his representative.

REXI's Impact on the City

The REXI resolution will directly affect the city in two important ways: one positive and one negative. First, the resolution threatens to reduce the city's economic base. Two of the three facilities targeted for the moratorium on expansion are located in Stillville. The other facility is located in Millville, the largest city in Portside County. Both of the Stillville facilities recently applied for zoning variances to allow for expansion of their facilities. They contend that world demand for their products is growing and the need for expansion is pressing. Together they employ just over 9,000 individuals and account for over one-half of all property taxes collected in Stillville, totaling $17 million.

The city's economic picture looks like this. Expenditures average about $45 million per year, and the city is running a deficit of approximately $2 million. It collects its revenues from the following sources: $30 million in property tax revenues, $1 million in sales taxes revenues, $3 million in tourism-related fees, and $6 million in city income taxes. The city also receives intergovernmental funds in the amount of $3 million.

The second effect of the REXI resolution is likely to be positive. A regional transportation hub in Stillville would support increased access to employment opportunities and job markets, provide jobs to transportation sector employees, and reduce vehicular air emissions. The reality is that the city's public transit service, which provides limited service, is almost bankrupt.

Stillville's city council must approve the REXI resolution. The mayor, who already voted for it, plans to meet with the council within the next month, to urge it to adopt the resolution and begin planning for its implementation. Domore has talked to the mayor on many occasions regarding the resolution, and they wholeheartedly agree that it would move the city toward sustainable development and benefit the entire region.

Council Politics

Beyond approval of the resolution, Domore needs the city council's approval of a budget that will allow the initiative's programs to succeed. In the past the council, excepting President Whitco, has shown interest in attracting new business to increase revenues, but it also has shown an interest in pursuing a sustainable approach. After the REXI resolution made the headlines, Whitco approached Domore to tell him that the city council would like a report detailing the REXI initiative for its meeting in two weeks. At the meeting Domore must present recommendations to the council on how to proceed.

In discussing the resolution with Domore, Whitco expressed frustration with the mayor's approach to solving Stillville's economic issues and his willingness to commit staff time to an initiative not yet reviewed by the council. More specifically, Whitco stated he would not tolerate city staff members' devoting additional time and energy to REXI activities. "The city staff should focus on local initiatives, and REXI membership strains valuable city resources," Whitco warned. "If Jane Environ remains on the committee and you do not limit her and others' involvement, I will begin the process of terminating your employment." This was Whitco's last statement to Domore.

After careful reflection, Domore concluded that his role as a city manager was to provide leadership, develop policy, and engage the community in improving the quality of life of the city's residents. He believed that the third role was clearly in concert with the mission of the city council. Now he would have to use his skills to convince Whitco that they share the same objective.

Whitco's unwillingness to commit staff resources to the initiative was due in part to his short-term (election period) focus. Domore perceived his responsibility, on the other hand, to extend not only to current but also to future residents. If he focused only on the needs and wants of those currently residing in the community, he strongly believed that the city's future quality of life would be jeopardized.

Domore thinks that by joining forces with other communities, Stillville will see long-term financial, social, ecological, and administrative benefits. For now, though, he needs more resources than the city has if he is to manage a midsized city faced with urban blight, declining prospects for economic growth, and high levels of air and water pollution. Coordination and collaboration are vital—so is reaching consensus among the parties within and outside the city. This approach could prove to be Domore's opportunity to moving the community into the twenty-first century in a sustainable way.

At the same time, Domore knows that if he is not responsive to the needs and desires of the city council, it has the authority to terminate him. While he brings a wealth of training and experience to the job, he is not irreplaceable. He also has a new baby on the way.

The Decision Problem

Richard Domore is now at the end of the two-week study period on the REXI initiative, and his report is nearly complete. The moratorium on industrial expansion and the public transit expansion project were evaluated separately. Table 1 summarizes the benefits and costs.

With the city council meeting less than two days away, Domore faces a set of critical questions before finalizing his recommendations:

1. How seriously, if at all, should he consider President Whitco's threat to terminate him?
2. Should he prepare a response to this threat or simply focus on the content of the presentation?
3. Given the lack of time to estimate the indirect benefits of improved human health and environmental quality, what is Domore's best method of presenting this information to the city council in a way that it will not dismiss these factors from its decision making?
4. How might he build a consensus for the initiative among city council members? Can he find a shared interest among all or the majority of the parties?
5. Does he need to take any additional actions prior to the council meeting? For example, should he talk with industry representatives, transportation representatives, or key leaders of citizens groups?

Domore also has a tentative list of recommendations, but he wonders whether he has identified all the most relevant options.

Possible Options

This is City Manager Domore's list of options.

1. The city council could support the initiative and begin to identify sources for the cost-sharing component of the rapid transit plan. The city staff would begin this work immediately. The council would also deny any requests, pending or future, for expansion for the next three years.

Table 1 Regional Excellence Initiative (REXI) Summary

	Benefits	Costs
Limited industrial expansion	• No deterioration in current human health (and possible improvement) • No increase in air and water pollution (and possible reduction)	• Loss of $2 million in additional property tax revenues per year • Loss of up to 400 new jobs • Loss of city income tax revenues in the amount of $200,000 per year
Expanded rapid transit with new hub	• Addition of up to 50 new transit jobs, and $100,000 in city income tax revenues per year • Increased access to jobs for Stillville citizens; an increase in city income tax revenues of $1 million per year • Sales tax revenue increase from additional spending in Stillville: $50,000 per year • State/federal funding of $5 million per year • Improved air quality; removal of EPA nonattainment designation for Northside County • Improved human health and productivity	• One-time cost-sharing contribution to the initiative in the amount of $5 million • Cost of renovating the current transportation center in the amount of $1.5 million for one year • Increased administrative costs of running transportation hub/system, totaling $500,000 per year

2. The city council could vote to postpone a decision on the initiative until after a thorough study of its costs and benefits, including those relating to environmental and human health improvements.
3. The city council could vote to postpone the decision indefinitely and hold a series of town hall meetings to solicit input from the citizens of Stillville.

Discussion Questions

1. What are the ethical implications of City Manager Richard Domore's choice? If he simply reported the facts, and recommended the council not endorse and participate in the initiative, would he violate the ICMA Code of Ethics?
2. How should Domore have responded to Whitco's threat to terminate him?
3. If we assume that Domore strongly recommends the first option in the case study, what supporting arguments can he draw on? Are there other examples that he might cite where urban blight was turned into prosperity?
4. What parties are needed to build consensus and move the initiative forward? For those in the community, what are the benefits of building consensus for this initiative?
5. What consensus-building techniques can Domore employ?
6. Are there measurable outcomes? Do measurable outcomes matter in consensus building?

Suggested Simulation Roles

City manager
City council president
City council
Mayor

Expanded Simulation Roles

REXI representative
Industry representative
Citizens

19

A Jail in City Center

Bill R. Adams, Glen W. Sparrow, and Ronald L. Ballard

Background

The residents of St. Regis County were whipped into a frenzy as news of jail overcrowding became public. The sheriff, Horace Farley, began beating the drums for a solution, claiming that the jails were powder kegs about to blow. More jails were needed now, or prisoners would have to be released onto the streets. Overcrowding was especially serious at the county's jail in the city of St. Regis.

The media, taking its cue from Farley, dutifully announced that there was indeed a jail crisis and that, of course, something must be done about it. The citizens concurred; something should be done. And so pressure was placed on the St. Regis County Board of Supervisors, the governing body charged with building jails for the entire county. The hysteria reached such a crescendo that the supervisors, who had neglected the issue for two decades, were compelled to declare the jail situation an emergency, and to calm mounting public frustration, county officials searched frantically for a quick-fix solution.

During the flap, citizens of the city of Rollins went about business as usual, unperturbed by the hubbub over villains and jail overcrowding. The jail issue was of marginal interest to Rollins residents, who were rarely visited by crime in their outlying city of 50,000. However, interest rose precipitously when the county declared Rollins to be the ideal spot for a new, temporary, six-hundred-bed men's jail. This proposal seemed reasonable to most of the county, which perceived Rollins as an outback, representing cowboys, country, western music, and people who did not mind long commutes. Rollins, as might be expected, became quite agitated at the decision, swearing to pit itself against the county juggernaut. Undaunted, the county reiterated its resolve to build, accusing the city of undermining "law and order" and obstructing a necessary solution to the problem. Both governments prepared for conflict.

And, indeed, they did fight. Events that led to this clash had been festering for about two decades. Eventually, the jail overcrowding became so bad that the American Civil Liberties Union filed a class-action suit on behalf of jail inmates. The U.S. District Court ultimately ruled that crowding in the county's city-of-St.-Regis jail was "cruel and unusual punishment" and ordered the sheriff and the county board of supervisors to find a solution to it. The search for a solution became even more urgent when the court imposed a 750-inmate cap on the facility.

There was no denying that the problem had become a monster because of the inaction of former boards. Lack of money, competing crises, and public dissatisfaction with earlier proposed solutions had allowed the issue to be continually set aside. Finally, the county responded by declaring a jail emergency and launching attempts to erect a temporary men's facility in the middle of Rollins, adjacent to the existing, but unobtrusive, women's jail.

The proposed jail was to be placed on county-owned land within the redevelopment area known as City Center, a project envisioned as the city's future commercial hub. The Rollins master plan called for a multiuse project focusing on a vibrant commercial core, pedestrian paths and walkways, lush landscaping, open space, fountains, and ponds—a dramatic recreational, commercial, and residential mix along the St. Regis River. For the city, this project was a matter of pride as well as of economic vitality. It was central to Rollins's attempt to show its sophistication, to overcome its "west-county cowboy" image, and to establish a solid commercial base that would carry it in relative economic comfort into the next century.

In contrast, the county was seeking a low-cost, low-conflict "fix" and, in the process, proposed a planner's nightmare: an open compound, warehousing six hundred inmates in ten barracks, and featuring dual chain-link fencing capped with coils of razor wire, guard towers, and minimal landscaping. From a marketing perspective, the facility could hardly be considered a draw for the 706-acre City Center redevelopment area.

The county's assurance that the facility would be temporary held no currency with the city. Aside from the county supervisors' refusal to give a definite termination date, there was little likelihood that, in the rapidly growing county, there would ever be enough empty beds to transfer six hundred or more inmates to other, yet-to-be-built facilities. Would the county give up an operating jail site, knowing that it was getting progressively harder to find communities willing to tolerate new jails? To Rollins, the answer was clearly no.

The problem confronting the city was what, if anything, could be done to derail the proposal? State law seemed to back the county's contention that it could erect anything without city approval if the land were used for public purposes. The irony was that a major reason for Rollins's incorporation years earlier had been to escape this type of external control. Legally, the county, owner of 371 acres in the northeastern sector of City Center, could destroy City Center by introducing all manner of unwanted public projects.

Rollins

It could be convincingly argued that Rollins, prior to its incorporation seven years earlier, had been a victim of benign neglect by the county of St. Regis, a neglect that had incited a revolt and sparked a home-rule movement in Rollins. The county's policy of approving strip zoning and high-density residential projects in Rollins had left a scar that became the major focus of city policy during Rollins's early postincorporation existence. Only time could heal much of the damage previously visited on the community by unpopular county land use decisions, but a well-planned downtown could be built from scratch in a relatively short period.

At the beginning of the 20th century, Rollins was a quiet, rural farming and dairy community, remaining so through World War II. It had taken the city almost seventy-five years to reach its 1950 population of 2,000. However, the winds of change struck as Rollins entered the late 1950s. To the chagrin of some and the glee of others (particularly developers), water and sewer lines were extended to the area, inviting development. Two water districts were formed in the region and eventually merged to become an independent special district, the Indian Valley Dam Municipal Water District. The Indian Valley Dam District provided both water and sewage treatment services for much of the urbanized western county, including Rollins.

In the 1950s, when the urbanization of Rollins began, a nebulous community began to take on a form dictated by topography. Except to the south, where the growing city of Rock Hill was located, large rocky hills isolated the Rollins valley from neighboring communities, including the city of St. Regis to the east, most of the sprawling community of Riverfront to the west, and the rugged northern lands. Soaring land values quickly transformed the farming community into a suburb, albeit a distant one, of downtown St. Regis. Land had simply become too expensive to farm. New homes and small shops began sprouting around the community of Rollins—projects marked by high density and strip zoning. Eventually, runaway growth and questionable planning ignited Rollins's home-rule movement.

As Rollins had evolved from a rural to an urban community, its leaders, disturbed by county actions, began to wonder whether county policy was indeed a form of benign neglect or a device to turn Rollins into a receptacle for projects shunned by other communities.

The idea of home rule continued to grow in popularity, and in 1980 voters approved Rollins's incorporation as one of sixteen municipalities in St. Regis County. Like all the other cities, it adopted the council-manager form of government.

The Creation of City Center

The center of Rollins was mostly vacant land surrounded by homes and small businesses. To Rollins's new city planners, it was almost too good to be true. Here was a chance to build a planned downtown—City Center—in a redevelopment area without first having to tear down existing structures. Adding to the lure was the St. Regis River, which bisected the property, making the land that much more attractive and valuable.

As one of its first major actions, the city council formed the Rollins Redevelopment Agency and became its policy board. Under state law, a city government, as a redevelopment agency, could issue bonds for revenue and use the proceeds to attract new development (through financial incentives) or otherwise improve a blighted or redevelopment area, hence increasing property values, quality of life, and the local tax base.

The declaration of City Center as a redevelopment area would freeze property tax revenues from the area for all governments (including the county). The bonds would be repaid through property tax increments accruing from upgraded property values, with all of the increment for the ensuing twenty years going to the redevelopment agency. In the case of Rollins, the redevelopment agency acquired $6.4 million in debt to ensure the success of City Center. If the project failed, the city would be responsible for the entire amount, plus interest.

With the redevelopment process defined, the Rollins Redevelopment Agency (the city council) went about the task of identifying the boundaries of City Center, which consisted of 706 contiguous acres of redevelopment land. This area included all of the property around two county facilities in the City Center area. One facility, Broadview, was the only county geriatric hospital and senior-citizens' home in St. Regis County. In 1966, across the street from Broadview, the county had opened Safe Haven, a "permanent" reform school for delinquent girls. The promise that it would remain a girls' reform school was breached a decade later when the structure was converted to a jail for women—the first and only one in the county.

As the 21st century dawned, the city began to tackle the tough questions concerning City Center land use. It took two hectic years for the city to approve a comprehensive land use package, called the City Center Specific Plan. During that period, the city council walked a thin line among groups of every political stripe: slow-growth advocates, free marketers, environmentalists, landowners, and developers. Getting everyone involved from the start and negotiating a comprehensive if compromise master plan was the city's strategy.

Complications

For the most part, the scheme worked for two years. The city held open meetings, discussions, workshops, conferences, and public hearings on City Center. At the start of the process the county and the city in a written pact agreed to plan City Center together. Had it not been for structural differences between the city and the county the cooperative planning venture for City Center might have worked. Both the city and the county had professional administrative leadership: the city with a city manager, Jerry Swanson, the county with a chief administrative officer, Jim Marshall. In theory, the resolution of differences between the city and the county should have been aided by negotiations between the city manager and the county administrator—professional peers.

The jurisdiction of the county administrator, however, was limited by the county's governmental structure, which provided for several elected administrative officers including the county sheriff. The governmental responsibilities assigned to the elected officers fell outside the purview of the administrator. While the administrator could and did attempt to work with and influence the elected officials, his influence varied. On politically sensitive matters the administrator frequently had limited influence with his elected colleagues.

The county jail was such a matter. Since the county's jails fell within the jurisdiction of the county sheriff, decisions regarding them were made by either the sheriff alone or the sheriff in consultation with the board of supervisors. Pressured by the courts, the press, local law enforcement agencies, and his own staff on the problem of jail overcrowding, Sheriff Farley was not inclined to work with the county administrator. He needed a new jail, he needed it now, and he was not going to waste time with what he regarded as extraneous concerns as he worked to get it. His ability to win reelection in a countywide race demanded that he resolve the jail crisis—and do it before the next election.

The Case

As the planning for City Center trudged along and the plan began to take form, the county—City Center's largest single landholder—objected to two related proposals: the amount of park and open space proposed on county land, and the resulting limits on the number of homes permitted on the remaining property. At first county officials protested quietly, but angered that the city was holding fast, they went public, airing their differences openly and in the press.

Two months later, the county announced its plans to build the men's jail in City Center, contending that the project did not require city approval because it was a public facility and not a commercial venture. The city was offended at the county's failure to notify it of the decision before going public. (As a courtesy, local agencies normally give advance notice when a policy decision will affect another's sphere of influence.) Tensions heightened when the city procured pictures of the type of facility planned (barracks, chain-link fencing, razor wire, guard towers) and made them public. However, by year's end, the city had persuaded the county to build elsewhere. A new study was completed, identifying an isolated area along the county's southern border as the new jail site. From outward appearances, Rollins had won.

A second confrontation, increasing the bad feelings between the county and Rollins, occurred a year later in a dispute over $1 million the county owed the city in unpaid tax moneys. Being short of cash, the county had proposed a swap of some of its City Center real estate to settle the debt. The city, wanting control over as much City Center land as possible, agreed, and a memorandum of understanding was signed by both parties. Unfortunately, they could not agree on the property's worth, and negotiations subsequently collapsed. Apparently agitated by the impasse, the county made a unilateral decision to retain the land and repay the debt in cash. An equally irritated city took the county to court for breach of contract, but lost.

The Jail Issue Resurfaces

Meanwhile, a storm was brewing in the city of St. Regis that would eventually affect Rollins. Because of jail overcrowding, the sheriff's department implemented a policy of book-and-release for misdemeanors, which included prostitution. Residents of neighborhoods with the greatest activity, however, complained to the city council that their streets were being overrun by prostitutes (and their potential customers) and that something had to be done. That sounded reasonable to the council, but what to do? Since all municipalities booked suspected criminals in the county jails, the city of St. Regis turned to the county. It decided to wave a carrot before the county supervisors: expand the women's detention facility at Safe Haven in Rollins so that more prostitutes could be locked up, and the city of St. Regis would cover half of the construction cost.

The county agreed. The Rollins city council, attempting to smooth ruffled feathers, decided to neither oppose nor support the expansion as long as it remained within the existing compound. The county agreed to Rollins's condition.

Nevertheless, fate dealt Rollins a double-cross when the board of supervisors, frustrated in its efforts to procure jail land in the proposed southern location, not only approved the expansion of the women's detention facility by almost two hundred beds but also ordered construction of the six-hundred-bed men's facility next door.

Rollins was stunned. Had this issue not been resolved less than a year earlier? The Rollins city council, angered by the county's behavior, gave City Manager Swanson a free hand, financially and otherwise, to defend the city from the threat.

Publicly, the county reasoned that the men's temporary jail could be built quickly next to Safe Haven (and removed after permanent facilities were built elsewhere) because the infrastructure—roads, electricity, water, and sewer capacity—was in place and the land already belonged to the county. Rumors that the jail was an excuse to punish Rollins for bucking the county on the City Center plan were denied.

The city argued the emotional issue of security: a male lockup located adjacent to homes, Broadview Hospital, and schools (Rollins Elementary School was only two blocks away) would present a real danger to the community and especially to the schoolchildren. The county waved off these concerns, saying that people would actually be safer with more sheriff's deputies in the area.

Although the county's response to safety issues was anticipated, city officials were puzzled by the county's inability to grasp the economic issue. Both jurisdictions had much to lose financially if the jail were built. With population on the rise in Rollins, healthy commercial development in City Center was needed to expand the city's tax base, which in turn would be used to maintain city services.

The jail, it was feared, could undo all efforts to attract upscale business to Rollins, thereby sinking City Center and conceivably the city's future. City leaders wondered why the county, which was always short of cash, would squander its extremely valuable City Center property on a project guaranteed to scare off money-making ventures. The county answered that the land was not that valuable anymore since a large segment of it had been zoned for park and open-space use. Furthermore, the county maintained, the jail would only be temporary and, after it was removed, land values would return to normal.

Crisis Management

To respond to the threat, a jail task force, made up of City Manager Swanson, the city attorney, and staff members, formulated a four-pronged strategy—political, administrative, public relations, and legal—all salted with a hefty dose of publicity. The city hoped to sandbag the project with delays—a tactic of attrition.

It fell to Jerry Swanson to provide the day-to-day management and coordination of the city's strategy. The city council took the lead on the political front, cajoling county officials and enlisting the aid of sympathetic politicians. The city staff undertook the task of managing the crisis administratively. This included doing technical work, tracking county actions, bird-dogging staff, attending meetings, studying jail-related documents, and publicizing via the media contrary city findings. A public information campaign involved the city's community services coordinator, city council members, and resident activists. It was decided that legal challenges would be used where and when necessary.

To assist in the preparation of its case, the city hired twelve consultants—experts in a range of fields including penal systems, criminology, ecosystems, flood control, fire regulations, socioeconomics, and public relations. The Rollins school board also lashed out at the county for suggesting the placement of a men's jail so near an elementary school attended by hundreds of children. The board members expressed concern over released and escaped prisoners, visitors, and increased traffic. The school district also hired a consultant to assist the city task force. Further, a Rollins citizens' anti-jail organization regrouped and turned up the heat on the county with letters, telephone calls, rallies, and picketing.

The first legal volley was fired when the city filed in county court for a restraining order, arguing that the county was preparing plans to build before completing an environmental impact report (EIR), as required by state law. This, the city argued, put the cart before the horse; that is, the county should not take steps to build in Rollins until the EIR was completed and had identified the best location for a jail. The county claimed it was following proper procedure—a contention with which the court eventually concurred.

At the same time, Rollins's mayor contacted local legislators and requested state legislation to put an end to the type of unilateral action undertaken by the county. But while legislators expressed sympathy, they introduced no legislation.

Another Government Gets Involved

At about the same time, the Indian Valley Dam District gave the county a scare with news that the sewer trunk line serving the district might be near capacity. If true, this announcement meant that the jail would have to be put on hold until the line was expanded, an action that could be years down the road. As it turned out, the line was near the limit but not close enough to halt the jail.

While the county went about the business of writing the EIR, the city opened negotiations with the Indian Valley Dam District for control of sewer lines in City Center. Under existing rules, sewer lines could be reserved from the Indian Valley Dam even if landowners had no intention of developing the land. Moreover, the agency sold sewer hookups on a first-come, first-served basis. Landowners merely had to prove ownership and possible future need for the sewer units requested. No city or county approval was necessary, as the Indian Valley Dam was an independent special district. (Sewer units are based on the average service one household requires: one sewer unit equals one household. The jail would require 112 units.)

Once reserved under the Indian Valley Dam scheme, sewer lines were locked to a particular property in perpetuity. This meant that a developer using less than the allotted quota was forbidden to resell, trade, or give away the remaining units to anyone else, including the dam district.

Because of the rapidly dwindling number of available units, the Indian Valley Dam's regulations could have wreaked havoc on City Center development, leaving certain parcels shy of units while others had a surfeit. Such a system had the potential of turning the City Center development into a game of chance, and Rollins had no intention of gambling with its future. Rollins proposed to the dam district that, because of its overriding interest, the city be granted control of the allocation of sewer capacity in the City Center area.

Two events had prompted the city's concern about City Center sewer lines. The first occurred when a major developer, who had become worried by published reports of diminishing sewer capacity, purchased almost half of the remaining sewer capacity (1,460 units) available to Rollins. That left Indian Valley Dam with only 833 units. The precipitous drop in available capacity alarmed Rollins officials, who saw the whole City Center project in jeopardy. The second event was the county jail proposal: the city would obviously gain significant leverage over the jail location if the county had to go through the city for sewer service.

The city argued before the Indian Valley Dam directors that, jail or no jail, the city must have authority over sewers in order to ensure the integrity of the City Center project. Following the presentation of Rollins's case, the Indian Valley Dam board chose to postpone a decision for two weeks. City officials, concerned that either private developers or the county would purchase the remaining sewer units, countered by requesting a moratorium on the sale of capacity for all locations until the next hearing. The city explained that it feared a "run" on the remaining hookups. Unconvinced, the board denied the request, leaving intact the first-come, first-served policy. County officials had noted in an earlier newspaper interview that they planned to reserve the 112 hookups necessary for the jail in "a day or two."

The Decision Problem

As he drove home from the meeting with the dam board, Swanson reviewed his handling of the crisis and concluded that time had run out. For two years the city had moved to keep the county from proceeding with a plan that would have seriously, and perhaps permanently, damaged Rollins's economic future. Plans had been created; support mobilized; research undertaken; legal, publicity, and political actions implemented; pleas made; and proposals put forward. Swanson realized, however, that the next morning he would have to act. Further, since there was no opportunity to meet with his council, any action he took would have to be rapid and unilateral.

The problem was more complicated than just stopping the county from proceeding with its plans to place the jail in City Center. While public opinion within Rollins strongly supported action to block the county, public opinion outside Rollins was running just as strongly in favor of the county's plan for the temporary jail location. Which public interest must be served—that of city residents or that of county residents? Although the manager served the city, the population of the county was many times larger than that of the city.

Still more factors were operating against the city. Rollins had lost on legal grounds in the court test; state legislation had not been forthcoming; other cities in St. Regis County had remained relatively silent lest the jail end up in their backyards; the county had the EIR, ownership of the property, and a federal district court order all going for it; and now the Indian Valley Dam board had chosen to vacillate rather than support the city.

The alternatives were limited; most avenues for relief were closed or rapidly closing. Reliance on other entities, judicial remedies, and political processes seemed to have been exhausted. If the county reserved the remaining sewer hookups, the city's cause would appear to have been lost. Yet no money had been appropriated by the city to pay the $600,000 required to reserve the hookups.

Was there anything Swanson should do? Was there anything he could do?

Discussion Questions

1. How should the manager define the public interest in this case? Which group of residents should take priority? Does the interest of the larger jurisdiction always take priority over that of the smaller jurisdiction? If so, why? If not, under what conditions should the smaller jurisdiction prevail?
2. What different governmental agencies are involved in this case? What are their interrelationships? In such a situation, what are the prerogatives of the city to protect the interests of its residents?
3. What principles should govern the behavior of the manager in this case? Which should take priority—his responsibility to his constituents, his commitment to democratic theory and representative government, or the laws of the city and the state? How should these be sorted out?
4. Does the issue under consideration affect the answer to the preceding questions? That is, when the public safety (retention in jail of those accused of crimes) conflicts with community control (the opportunity for economic and land use enhancement), which should take precedence and why?
5. What interpretation would you put on the council's direction that the manager act with "a free hand, financially and otherwise," to defend the city? Does such an authorization enable the manager to spend money without an appropriation? How far does it go in justifying unilateral action by the manager?
6. Given that he is unable to meet with the city council (and regardless of the answer to question 5), are there other efforts at consultation that Swanson ought to make before he acts? If so, what are they?
7. Do the time constraints faced in this situation produce "emergency" conditions? Do such conditions permit the manager to exceed his usual authority? If so, by how much? If not, how does a manager defend governmental inaction in the face of emergency situations?
8. Are there situations in which the urgent need for action justifies a government, or an administrator, ignoring accepted and "normal" procedures and engaging in "guerrilla warfare"? Does this situation, with its long-term economic implications, justify such behavior?
9. What tactical options are available to Swanson? What option should he choose? How can it be defended?

Suggested Simulation Roles

Jerry Swanson, city manager
Staff assistant
City attorney (optional)
City community services coordinator
City finance director

About the Authors and Editor*

Bill R. Adams (Case 19) served as public information officer for a decade with the city of Santee in San Diego County. He has also worked in news and information in the private sector, covering local politics in Washington, D.C., and San Diego; has taught; and has been a publications and Internet consultant. He earned a bachelor's degree from the University of Maryland at College Park.

Ronald L. Ballard (Case 19) served for fifteen years as city manager for Santee, a fast-growing San Diego County municipality. Before retiring in 1997, he held positions with several other California cities, including the position of assistant city manager in National City. He holds a master's degree in public administration from San Diego State University and a bachelor's degree from Bethany College, Santa Cruz.

Julie Car (Case 10) is a planner III in the Long Range Planning section of the Planning and Community Development Department for the county of Sacramento. She is on the Open Space Team and is working on projects related to flood control, levee improvements, and wildlife habitat conservation. She has a master's degree in urban and regional planning and a bachelor of science degree in fisheries and wildlife from Michigan State University.

Larry M. Comunale (Case 1) is the township manager in Lower Gwynedd Township, Montgomery County, Pennsylvania. He is a past president of the Montgomery County Municipal Managers Consortium and is president of the Association of Pennsylvania Municipal Management. He also serves on the board of directors of the Montgomery County Association of Township Officials. He has taught numerous seminars for municipal officials and is an adjunct professor with Villanova University's M.P.A. program. Comunale received his B.S. degree and master's degree in public administration from the Pennsylvania State University.

Victoria Gordon (Case 2 and Case 12) is an assistant professor in the political science department at Western Kentucky University. She also serves as director for the Center for Local Governments, which provides training and research services to cities and counties in Kentucky. Dr. Gordon holds a D.P.A. from the University of Illinois at Springfield and an M.P.A. from the University of Kansas. Dr. Gordon has many years of experience in local government management at the city and county level, which complements her primary research interests, including human resource management and regional economic development.

Jerry Kloby (Case 7) is an assistant professor of sociology at the County College of Morris in New Jersey. He is active in a number of organizations working on community building and affordable housing. In addition, his areas of interests include community studies, inequality, and globalization. Dr. Kloby is the author

*Information about Adams, Ballard, and Mills is as of the publication date of *Managing Local Government: Cases in Decision Making,* 2nd edition (1998), in which their cases also appeared.

of *Inequality, Power, and Development: Issues in Political Sociology.* His current research examines practical techniques and management approaches to address shrinking cities and urban regeneration as demonstrated in Leinfelde, in the former East Germany.

Kathryn Kloby (Case 15) is an assistant professor of political science at Monmouth University. Her research interests include public sector accountability, government performance measurement and reporting, and citizen participation. She has published several articles and book chapters examining initiatives that increase the overlap between government decisions and citizen expectations. Dr. Kloby's current research addresses the potential for community indicator projects to more closely align their efforts with government-sponsored performance measurement projects.

Scott D. Lazenby (Case 4 and Case 16) has been city manager of Sandy, Oregon, since 1992. Prior to that, he served as management and budget director for the city of Glendale, Arizona, and assistant to the city manager for Vancouver, Washington. He has a bachelor's degree in physics from Reed College and a master of science degree in public policy and management from Carnegie Mellon University. He is working on a Ph.D. in public administration at Portland State University. A past president of the Oregon City/County Management Association, he authored the novel *Playing with Fire.*

Jack Manahan (Case 6) is the chief financial officer of the Unified Government of Wyandotte County/Kansas City, Kansas. He has held positions in city and county management in Kansas and Illinois and was a senior consultant with an international technology consulting firm. He was a member of the National Advisory Council on State and Local Budgeting and a member of the Government Finance Officers Association's Governmental Budgeting and Fiscal Policy Committee. He is past chair of the ICMA Academic Affairs Task Force and a former board member of the Illinois City/County Management Association. He has a master's degree in public administration from the University of Kansas.

Tom Mills (Case 14) has been director of executive education at the Fels Institute of Government, University of Pennsylvania. A former city official in Philadelphia for twenty-two years, he served the city as deputy managing director, chief deputy court administrator, and first deputy finance director. He has held positions at Fairleigh Dickinson University (Rutherford campus), Trenton State College, and Temple University.

Leighann Moffitt (Case 10) is principal planner in the Sacramento County Planning and Community Development Department, managing the countywide planning team responsible for the update of key planning documents for the jurisdiction, including those covering the general plan, housing, habitat conservation, river parkway, and a joint vision project. She holds a combined bachelor of science degree in business administration management and environmental studies from California State University, Sacramento. She is a member of the American Planning Association and the American Institute of Certified Planners.

Charldean Newell (editor) is regents professor emerita of public administration at the University of North Texas, where her teaching, research, and numerous publications focused on local government management and Texas politics. She held four administrative positions. A fellow of the National Academy of Public Administration and an honorary member of ICMA, Newell serves on the Credentialing Advisory Board and teaches in the Emerging Leaders Program. She has chaired a charter revision committee, the Fire and Police Civil Service Board, and the Public Utilities Board in her community and served on the city council ethics committee.

Susan M. Opp (Case 3) is an assistant professor of public administration and co-director of the M.P.A. program at Texas Tech University. She received her Ph.D. in urban and public affairs at the University of Louisville in 2007. Dr. Opp's areas of expertise include environmental policy, sustainable development, and policy analysis.

Saundra Reinke (Case 11) is an associate professor and director of the M.P.A. program in the Department of Political Science at Augusta State University. She earned her D.P.A from the University of Alabama. She has authored seven articles in peer-reviewed journals, two case studies, several book reviews, and three book chapters. She introduced service-learning into the M.P.A. curriculum and has directed her students in a total of fifteen service-learning projects, benefiting twelve different government and nonprofit agencies in the Central Savannah River Area. She was ordained a deacon in the Episcopal Church in 2003, and her ministry focus is Epiphany, a program to reach incarcerated youth.

Carmine Scavo (Case 5) is an associate professor of political science and public administration at East Carolina University. He earned his Ph.D. in political science from the University of Michigan. He routinely teaches both graduate and undergraduate courses in municipal administration, urban politics, state and local government, and intergovernmental relations. His work has appeared in journals such as *Public Administration Review, Urban Affairs Review,* and *The Journal of Urban Affairs* as well as in edited volumes.

Gary L. Sears (Cases 8 and 17) is city manager of Englewood, Colorado. A public manager for over thirty-five years, he is past president of the Colorado City County Management Association and the Colorado Municipal League. He received the Leo G. Reithmeyer Award from the University of Colorado in 2002 as the Public Administrator of the Year. Sears is an adjunct professor with the University of Colorado's Graduate School of Political Science and a member of the Commission on Peer Review and Accreditation for the National Association of Schools of Public Affairs and Administration. Sears has a bachelor's degree from Monmouth College and a master's of public administration degree from the University of Colorado.

Glen W. Sparrow (Case 19) is professor emeritus at the School of Public Administration and Urban Studies, San Diego State University. His areas of specialization include state and local management and intergovernmental relations. He has been executive director of the Sacramento and San Francisco charter commissions and director of a Comprehensive Employment and Training Act prime sponsor. He has also been a consultant to cities and counties in California, especially in the area of incorporation, fiscal impact, and public-private partnerships. He has lectured and consulted at universities in Hong Kong, Canada, Mexico, and Hungary.

June S. Speakman (Case 9) is the Wilf Professor of Political Science at Roger Williams University in Bristol, Rhode Island, where she teaches American politics and public administration. She has a Ph.D. in political science from City University of New York and an M.A. in economics from the New School for Social Research. She has been involved in service to her community for almost fifteen years, starting with local parent-teacher organizations. She is serving her second term on her local town council.

Ellen Szarleta-Yancy (Case 18) is an assistant professor in the Division of Public and Environmental Affairs at Indiana University Northwest. She earned her Ph.D. in economics from the University of Wisconsin and her J.D. from the University of Iowa. She has worked in the area of environmental policy and economic development for over twenty years, focusing specifically on the study of federal and local environmental decision-making processes. Her most recent research examines the intersection of environmental law and sustainable development principles in the reclamation of contaminated sites. She also has examined the role of citizen participation in formulating state public notification plans for beach and coastal advisory programs.

Craig M. Wheeland (Case 1) is professor of political science at Villanova University. He received an M.P.A. from the University of South Carolina and a Ph.D. from the Pennsylvania State University. He serves as associate vice president for academic affairs. His research interests include leadership by elected officials and professional administrators in city and suburban governments, collaborative problem-solving approaches, and municipal government institutions. He has published articles in leading academic journals and numerous chapters in edited books, especially with ICMA. He is author of *Empowering the Vision: Community-Wide Strategic Planning in Rock Hill, South Carolina,* published by University Press of America.

M.P.A. students (Case 13) at the University of Wisconsin/Oshkosh who collaborated to produce a case are: **Tim Styka,** bachelor's degree in business administration from St. Norbert College (1993); **April Konitzer,** bachelor of science degree in business administration at University of Wisconsin/Green Bay (1989); **Michael Richards,** bachelor of arts in political science and legal studies at University of Wisconsin/Eau Claire (2000); **Derek Jablonicky,** bachelor of science in political science and public administration from University of Wisconsin/Stevens Point (2006); and **Lea Kitz,** bachelor of science in social work at University of Wisconsin/Oshkosh (1984).

ICMA Code of Ethics

With Guidelines

The ICMA Code of Ethics was adopted by the ICMA membership in 1924, and most recently amended by the membership in May 1998. The Guidelines for the Code were adopted by the ICMA Executive Board in 1972, and most recently revised in July 2004.

The mission of ICMA is to create excellence in local governance by developing and fostering professional local government management worldwide. To further this mission, certain principles, as enforced by the Rules of Procedure, shall govern the conduct of every member of ICMA, who shall:

1. Be dedicated to the concepts of effective and democratic local government by responsible elected officials and believe that professional general management is essential to the achievement of this objective.
2. Affirm the dignity and worth of the services rendered by government and maintain a constructive, creative, and practical attitude toward local government affairs and a deep sense of social responsibility as a trusted public servant.

   Guideline

   Advice to Officials of Other Local Governments. When members advise and respond to inquiries from elected or appointed officials of other local governments, they should inform the administrators of those communities.
3. Be dedicated to the highest ideals of honor and integrity in all public and personal relationships in order that the member may merit the respect and confidence of the elected officials, of other officials and employees, and of the public.

   Guidelines

   Public Confidence. Members should conduct themselves so as to maintain public confidence in their profession, their local government, and in their performance of the public trust.

   Impression of Influence. Members should conduct their official and personal affairs in such a manner as to give the clear impression that they cannot be improperly influenced in the performance of their official duties.

   Appointment Commitment. Members who accept an appointment to a position should not fail to report for that position. This does not preclude the possibility of a member considering several offers or seeking several positions at the same time, but once a *bona fide* offer of a position has been accepted, that commitment should be honored. Oral acceptance of an employment offer is considered binding unless the employer makes fundamental changes in terms of employment.

Credentials. An application for employment or for ICMA's Voluntary Credentialing Program should be complete and accurate as to all pertinent details of education, experience, and personal history. Members should recognize that both omissions and inaccuracies must be avoided.

Professional Respect. Members seeking a management position should show professional respect for persons formerly holding the position or for others who might be applying for the same position. Professional respect does not preclude honest differences of opinion; it does preclude attacking a person's motives or integrity in order to be appointed to a position.

Reporting Ethics Violations. When becoming aware of a possible violation of the ICMA Code of Ethics, members are encouraged to report the matter to ICMA. In reporting the matter, members may choose to go on record as the complainant or report the matter on a confidential basis.

Confidentiality. Members should not discuss or divulge information with anyone about pending or completed ethics cases, except as specifically authorized by the Rules of Procedure for Enforcement of the Code of Ethics.

Seeking Employment. Members should not seek employment for a position having an incumbent administrator who has not resigned or been officially informed that his or her services are to be terminated.

4. Recognize that the chief function of local government at all times is to serve the best interests of all of the people.

   Guideline

   Length of Service. A minimum of two years generally is considered necessary in order to render a professional service to the local government. A short tenure should be the exception rather than a recurring experience. However, under special circumstances, it may be in the best interests of the local government and the member to separate in a shorter time. Examples of such circumstances would include refusal of the appointing authority to honor commitments concerning conditions of employment, a vote of no confidence in the member, or severe personal problems. It is the responsibility of an applicant for a position to ascertain conditions of employment. Inadequately determining terms of employment prior to arrival does not justify premature termination.

5. Submit policy proposals to elected officials; provide them with facts and advice on matters of policy as a basis for making decisions and setting community goals; and uphold and implement local government policies adopted by elected officials.

   Guideline

   Conflicting Roles. Members who serve multiple roles—working as both city attorney and city manager for the same community, for example—should avoid participating in matters that create the appearance of a conflict of interest. They should disclose the potential conflict to the governing body so that other opinions may be solicited.

6. Recognize that elected representatives of the people are entitled to the credit for the establishment of local government policies; responsibility for policy execution rests with the members.

7. Refrain from all political activities which undermine public confidence in professional administrators. Refrain from participation in the election of the members of the employing legislative body.

Guidelines

Elections of the Governing Body. Members should maintain a reputation for serving equally and impartially all members of the governing body of the local government they serve, regardless of party. To this end, they should not engage in active participation in the election campaign on behalf of or in opposition to candidates for the governing body.

Elections of Elected Executives. Members should not engage in the election campaign of any candidate for mayor or elected county executive.

Running for Office. Members shall not run for elected office or become involved in political activities related to running for elected office. They shall not seek political endorsements, financial contributions or engage in other campaign activities.

Elections. Members share with their fellow citizens the right and responsibility to vote and to voice their opinion on public issues. However, in order not to impair their effectiveness on behalf of the local governments they serve, they shall not participate in political activities to support the candidacy of individuals running for any city, county, special district, school, state or federal offices. Specifically, they shall not endorse candidates, make financial contributions, sign or circulate petitions, or participate in fund-raising activities for individuals seeking or holding elected office.

Elections on the Council-Manager Plan. Members may assist in preparing and presenting materials that explain the council-manager form of government to the public prior to an election on the use of the plan. If assistance is required by another community, members may respond. All activities regarding ballot issues should be conducted within local regulations and in a professional manner.

Presentation of Issues. Members may assist the governing body in presenting issues involved in referenda such as bond issues, annexations, and similar matters.

8. Make it a duty continually to improve the member's professional ability and to develop the competence of associates in the use of management techniques.

   Guidelines

   Self-Assessment. Each member should assess his or her professional skills and abilities on a periodic basis.

   Professional Development. Each member should commit at least 40 hours per year to professional development activities that are based on the practices identified by the members of ICMA.

9. Keep the community informed on local government affairs; encourage communication between the citizens and all local government officers; emphasize friendly and courteous service to the public; and seek to improve the quality and image of public service.

10. Resist any encroachment on professional responsibilities, believing the member should be free to carry out official policies without interference, and handle each problem without discrimination on the basis of principle and justice.

    Guideline

    Information Sharing. The member should openly share information with the governing body while diligently carrying out the member's responsibilities as set forth in the charter or enabling legislation.

11. Handle all matters of personnel on the basis of merit so that fairness and impartiality govern a member's decisions pertaining to appointments, pay adjustments, promotions, and discipline.

Guideline

Equal Opportunity. All decisions pertaining to appointments, pay adjustments, promotions, and discipline should prohibit discrimination because of race, color, religion, sex, national origin, sexual orientation, political affiliation, disability, age, or marital status.

It should be the members' personal and professional responsibility to actively recruit and hire a diverse staff throughout their organizations.

12. Seek no favor; believe that personal aggrandizement or profit secured by confidential information or by misuse of public time is dishonest.

Guidelines

Gifts. Members should not directly or indirectly solicit any gift or accept or receive any gift—whether it be money, services, loan, travel, entertainment, hospitality, promise, or any other form—under the following circumstances: (1) it could be reasonably inferred or expected that the gift was intended to influence them in the performance of their official duties; or (2) the gift was intended to serve as a reward for any official action on their part.

It is important that the prohibition of unsolicited gifts be limited to circumstances related to improper influence. In *de minimus* situations, such as meal checks, some modest maximum dollar value should be determined by the member as a guideline. The guideline is not intended to isolate members from normal social practices where gifts among friends, associates, and relatives are appropriate for certain occasions.

Investments in Conflict with Official Duties. Member should not invest or hold any investment, directly or indirectly, in any financial business, commercial, or other private transaction that creates a conflict with their official duties.

In the case of real estate, the potential use of confidential information and knowledge to further a member's personal interest requires special consideration. This guideline recognizes that members' official actions and decisions can be influenced if there is a conflict with personal investments. Purchases and sales which might be interpreted as speculation for quick profit ought to be avoided (see the guideline on "Confidential Information").

Because personal investments may prejudice or may appear to influence official actions and decisions, members may, in concert with their governing body, provide for disclosure of such investments prior to accepting their position as local government administrator or prior to any official action by the governing body that may affect such investments.

Personal Relationships. Members should disclose any personal relationship to the governing body in any instance where there could be the appearance of a conflict of interest. For example, if the manager's spouse works for a developer doing business with the local government, that fact should be disclosed.

Confidential Information. Members should not disclose to others, or use to further their personal interest, confidential information acquired by them in the course of their official duties.

Private Employment. Members should not engage in, solicit, negotiate for, or promise to accept private employment, nor should they render services for private interests or conduct a private business when such employment, service, or business creates a conflict with or impairs the proper discharge of their official duties.

Teaching, lecturing, writing, or consulting are typical activities that may not involve conflict of interest, or impair the proper discharge of their official duties. Prior notification of the appointing authority is appropriate in all cases of outside employment.

Representation. Members should not represent any outside interest before any agency, whether public or private, except with the authorization of or at the direction of the appointing authority they serve.

Endorsements. Members should not endorse commercial products or services by agreeing to use their photograph, endorsement, or quotation in paid or other commercial advertisements, whether or not for compensation. Members may, however, agree to endorse the following, provided they do not receive any compensation: (1) books or other publications; (2) professional development or educational services provided by nonprofit membership organizations or recognized educational institutions; (3) products and/or services in which the local government has a direct economic interest.

Members' observations, opinions, and analyses of commercial products used or tested by their local governments are appropriate and useful to the profession when included as part of professional articles and reports.

MANAGING LOCAL GOVERNMENT: Cases in Effectiveness

Design and layout: Will Kemp
Text type: Slimbach, Interstate

Printer: United Book Press